Study Notes on
Basic Bible Truth

(6) As ye have therefore received Christ Jesus the Lord, *so* walk ye in him: (7) Rooted and built up in him, and stablished in the faith, as ye have been taught, abounding therein with thanksgiving. (Col. 2:6-7)

David O'Steen

All Rights Reserved

No part of this book may be reproduced, or stored in a retrieval system, or transmitted in any form or by any means, electronic, mechanical, photocopying, recording, or otherwise, without express written permission of the publisher.

First Printed in November 2021

ISBN: 9798762439428
Printed in the United States of America

The Study Notes Series

The *skeleton* of information in the Study Notes series is compiled from my personal Bible study notes. I have been working to *put some meat on the bones* in an effort to make the notes more readable for others. These books are not wordy commentaries, but they are more than just a collection of outlines.

This book is designed to function as a study guide and companion to our video series on Basic Bible Truth (go to www.hopebiblechurchga.com and click on Video under Resources).

All scripture references are taken from the Authorized King James Bible. The final authority is the word of God (2 Tim. 3:16). Please take the time to search the scriptures and see whether these things are so (Acts 17:11; 1 Thess. 5:21).

It is my heart's desire and prayer that God will use this book for His glory and the edification of the saints.

And now, brethren, I commend you to God, and to the word of his grace, which is able to build you up, and to give you an inheritance among all them which are sanctified. (Acts 20:32)

David O'Steen
Jackson, Georgia

Table of Contents

Introduction 5
1. Salvation 8
2. Knowing God 15
3. The Bible 25
4. Following Christ Through Paul 34
5. Prayer 40
6. The Church 47
7. The Believer's Two Natures 55
8. Law and Grace 63
9. Standing and State 71
10. The Will of God 79
11. Our Commission 84
12. Our Enemies 91
13. Suffering 100
14. Our Blessed Hope 108
The Most Important Question 117

Introduction

The word of God is likened to food because without it we cannot be spiritually healthy and strong.

- Bread (Matt. 4:4)
- Honey (Ps. 119:103)
- Milk (1 Pet. 2:2)
- Meat (Heb. 5:12-14)

(6) If thou put the brethren in remembrance of these things, thou shalt be a good minister of Jesus Christ, <u>nourished</u> up in the words of faith and of good doctrine, whereunto thou hast attained.
(7) But <u>refuse</u> profane and old wives' fables, and <u>exercise</u> thyself *rather* unto godliness.
(8) For bodily exercise profiteth little: but godliness is profitable unto all things, having promise of the life that now is, and of that which is to come. (1 Tim. 4:6-8)

As with our physical body, there are three keys to spiritual health.

1) Nourishment in sound doctrine
2) Refusal of false doctrine
3) Exercise in godliness

(16) All scripture *is* given by inspiration of God, and *is* profitable for doctrine, for reproof, for correction, for instruction in righteousness:
(17) That the man of God may be perfect, throughly furnished unto all good works. (2 Tim. 3:16-17)

The Spirit of God gives believers an appetite for the word of God. To grow spiritually, we must personally eat (by reading and studying) and digest (by believing and meditating) the word of God.

Thy words were found, and I did eat them; and thy word was unto me the joy and rejoicing of mine heart: for I am called by thy name, O LORD God of hosts. (Jer. 15:16)

The apostle Paul distinguished between the milk (i.e., basics) and meat (i.e., deeper things) of the word of God in relation to three types of believers.

(1) And I, brethren, could not speak unto you as unto spiritual, but as unto carnal, *even* as unto babes in Christ.
(2) I have fed you with milk, and not with meat: for hitherto ye were not able *to bear it,* neither yet now are ye able.
(3) For ye are yet carnal: for whereas *there is* among you envying, and strife, and divisions, are ye not carnal, and walk as men? (1 Cor. 3:1-3)

The "natural man" (1 Cor. 2:14) is one who does not have the Spirit of God and therefore cannot receive the spiritual things of God.

For ye are all the children of God by faith in Christ Jesus.
(Gal. 3:26)

As to our standing before God, all believers are complete in Christ the moment of salvation (Col. 2:10), but as to our practical state we must grow spiritually.

Among the saved, there are:
1) **Babes** – New believers who must begin with the milk of the word.
2) **Spiritual** – Those who have grown spiritually to the point of being able to digest the meat of the word (1 Cor. 2:6-16). That we are able to eat the meat of the word does not mean that we no longer need the milk. Reviewing the basics is good even for mature saints.
3) **Carnal** – The scripture rebukes believers who remain as babes when they should be growing into spiritual maturity. Carnal believers are identified by their walk. They have access to the truth of God's word but have not received the proper nourishment from it which is evident by the fact it does not impact how they live. They walk after the flesh instead of in the Spirit.

We are all at different points in our spiritual growth. Whether you are a babe, spiritual, or carnal, the lessons in this book will be a benefit to you.

Chapter 1
Salvation

We will begin with a simple lesson on salvation because unless a person is saved, they cannot learn the spiritual truth of God's word. It is also important for believers to have the assurance of salvation. Those who struggle with doubts about salvation will not grow spiritually.

What Salvation Means

The word "salvation" appears 164 times in the Bible and basically means deliverance.

(34) O give thanks unto the LORD; for *he is* good; for his mercy *endureth* for ever.
(35) And say ye, <u>Save us</u>, O God of <u>our salvation</u>, and gather us together, and <u>deliver us</u> from the heathen, that we may give thanks to thy holy name, *and* glory in thy praise.
(36) Blessed *be* the LORD God of Israel for ever and ever. And all the people said, Amen, and praised the LORD.
(1 Chron. 16:34-36)

In this lesson we are not talking about being delivered from physical and temporary danger, but from spiritual and eternal danger.

**(16) For I am not ashamed of the gospel of Christ: for it is the power of God unto salvation to every one that believeth; to the Jew first, and also to the Greek.
(17) For therein is the righteousness of God revealed from faith to faith: as it is written, The just shall live by faith.
(18) For the wrath of God is revealed from heaven against all ungodliness and unrighteousness of men, who hold the truth in unrighteousness;** (Rom. 1:16-18)

Salvation is a deliverance both FROM and UNTO some things.

1) From Satan unto God (Acts 26:18)
2) From darkness unto light (Col. 1:13)
3) From hell unto heaven (Eph. 2:4-7)
4) From death unto life (Eph. 2:1)
5) From sin unto righteousness (2 Cor. 5:21)
6) From bondage of the law unto liberty (Rom. 7:6)
7) From the world unto the Body of Christ (Gal. 1:4)

Why Salvation is Needed

God created man in His own image (Gen. 1:27). Having a free will, man needed to be tested (Gen. 2:15-17). Adam fell when he disobeyed the word of God (Rom. 5:12). All who are born into this world are born of fallen and corrupt flesh (Rom. 3:10-19). All personally choose to sin and are responsible before God.

For the wages of sin *is* death; but the gift of God *is* eternal life through Jesus Christ our Lord. (Rom. 6:23)

Death is not annihilation, but separation. There are different kinds of death mentioned in the Bible.

1) Spiritual death (Eph. 2:1) – The lost are separated from the Spirit of God.
2) Physical death (Heb. 9:27) – The soul and spirit depart the body upon physical death.
3) Second death (Rev. 20:14-15) – Those who die lost will be separated from God in the lake of fire for eternity.

Who Accomplished Salvation

Salvation is not in religion, but in the Lord Jesus Christ who came down from heaven about 2,000 years ago to save sinners (1 Tim. 1:15). How did Jesus Christ accomplish salvation? God is righteous. Therefore, sin must be punished. In amazing love, the sinless Son of God willingly died on the cross for our sins, was buried, and rose again the third day in victory over sin, death, and the Devil.

(1) Moreover, brethren, I declare unto you the gospel which I preached unto you, which also ye have received, and wherein ye stand;
(2) By which also ye are saved, if ye keep in memory what I preached unto you, unless ye have believed in vain.
(3) For I delivered unto you first of all that which I also received, how that Christ died for our sins according to the scriptures;
(4) And that he was buried, and that he rose again the third day according to the scriptures: (1 Cor. 15:1-4)

Salvation is now offered as a FREE GIFT to all who will receive it (Rom. 5:18; 6:23).

How Salvation is Received

When a sinner realizes their lost condition and hears the gospel of salvation, the only thing they must do to be saved is trust in the finished work of Jesus Christ. Faith is simply believing what God said (Rom. 10:17).

In whom ye also *trusted,* after that ye heard the word of truth, the gospel of your salvation: in whom also after that ye believed, ye were sealed with that holy Spirit of promise, (Eph. 1:13)

(8) For by grace are ye saved through faith; and that not of yourselves: *it is* the gift of God:
(9) Not of works, lest any man should boast. (Eph. 2:8-9)

To believe that you must also do works, such as water baptism, means that you have not believed the gospel of the grace of God (Acts 20:24; 1 Cor. 1:17) and trusted in the finished work of Christ.

Not by works of righteousness which we have done, but according to his mercy he saved us, by the washing of regeneration, and renewing of the Holy Ghost; (Titus 3:5)

Since salvation is in Christ alone, we can know for sure that we are saved because He cannot lie or fail (2 Tim. 1:12; Titus 1:2). God wants believers to enjoy "much assurance" concerning salvation (1 Thess. 1:5). Assurance is based on the word of God, not on how we feel or live.

What Salvation Includes

We are saved the moment we trust Christ, but we will spend the rest of our life learning all that we received in Christ.

Blessed *be* the God and Father of our Lord Jesus Christ, who hath blessed us with all spiritual blessings in heavenly *places* in Christ: (Eph. 1:3)

There are many important doctrines to learn that pertain to salvation such as redemption, reconciliation, regeneration, and adoption.

There are three tenses of salvation.

1) **Past** – We were JUSTIFIED when we believed the gospel (Rom. 5:1). Justification means that we are righteous in the sight of God. We are saved from penalty of sin.

2) **Present** – As we grow spiritually, we learn how to live a SANCTIFIED life (Jn. 17:17). Sanctification means that we are set apart for God. We are being saved from the power of sin in our daily walk.

3) **Future** – When Christ comes for His church, we will be GLORIFIED in His image (Phil. 3:20-21). Glorification means that we will never sin again. We will be saved from the presence of sin.

We were spiritually baptized by the Holy Spirit into the church which is the Body of Christ the moment we believed the gospel.

For by one Spirit are we all baptized into one body, whether *we be* Jews or Gentiles, whether *we be* bond or free; and have been all made to drink into one Spirit. (1 Cor. 12:13)

The Holy Spirit seals unto the day we receive our glorified body.

And grieve not the holy Spirit of God, whereby ye are sealed unto the day of redemption. (Eph. 4:30)

Being a member of the Body of Christ and sealed with the Spirit means that we have eternal security and can never lose salvation.

(38) For I am persuaded, that neither death, nor life, nor angels, nor principalities, nor powers, nor things present, nor things to come,
(39) Nor height, nor depth, nor any other creature, shall be able to separate us from the love of God, which is in Christ Jesus our Lord. (Rom. 8:38-39)

This truth will motivate the sincere believer to serve God and not to continue living in sin.

(1) What shall we say then? Shall we continue in sin, that grace may abound?
(2) God forbid. How shall we, that are dead to sin, live any longer therein? (Rom. 6:1-2)

Chapter 1
Review Questions

1. List three things that salvation is a deliverance from and unto:
   1) From _____ Unto _____
   2) From _____ Unto _____
   3) From _____ Unto _____

2. Who needs salvation and why?

3. Who accomplished salvation and how did He do it?

4. Are there any works that we must do to receive salvation?

5. What are the three tenses of salvation?
   1) _____
   2) _____
   3) _____

Chapter 2
Knowing God

Salvation is about more than going to Heaven when we die. It is about knowing God and enjoying a real relationship with Him.

And this is life eternal, that they might know thee the only true God, and Jesus Christ, whom thou hast sent. (Jn. 17:3)

God saved us for Himself that we might know Him, worship Him, walk with Him, and serve Him.

For if, when we were enemies, we were reconciled to God by the death of his Son, much more, being reconciled, we shall be saved by his life. (Rom. 5:10)

And all things *are* of God, who hath reconciled us to himself by Jesus Christ, and hath given to us the ministry of reconciliation; (2 Cor. 5:18)

Who gave himself for us, that he might redeem us from all iniquity, and purify unto himself a peculiar people, zealous of good works. (Titus 2:14)

For most people, the purpose of life is a great mystery. What a blessing it is to know what our purpose is!

Thou art worthy, O Lord, to receive glory and honour and power: for thou hast created all things, and for thy pleasure they are and were created. (Rev. 4:11)

In the beginning God created Adam in His own image and walked with him in the garden.

So God created man in his *own* image, in the image of God created he him; male and female created he them. (Gen. 1:27)

When man sinned against God he died spiritually (Eph. 2:1) and was separated from God.

And they heard the voice of the LORD God walking in the garden in the cool of the day: and Adam and his wife <u>hid themselves from the presence of the LORD God</u> amongst the trees of the garden. (Gen. 3:8)

However, in Christ the believer has been renewed in God's image and can therefore know Him.

And have put on the new *man,* which is renewed in knowledge after the image of him that created him: (Col. 3:10)

In eternity, all of the redeemed will dwell with God as He originally intended, which proves that our main purpose for existence is to know God and walk with Him.

(3) And I heard a great voice out of heaven saying, Behold, the tabernacle of God *is* with men, and he will

**dwell with them, and they shall be his people, and God himself shall be with them, *and be* their God.
(4) And God shall wipe away all tears from their eyes; and there shall be no more death, neither sorrow, nor crying, neither shall there be any more pain: for the former things are passed away.
(5) And he that sat upon the throne said, Behold, I make all things new. And he said unto me, Write: for these words are true and faithful.** (Rev. 21:3-5)

That we may know God is a great privilege that we should never take lightly. False gods, such as Allah (Islam), are unknowable because they are not real. Christianity is the only faith that teaches that it is possible to have a personal relationship with God.

There is one true and living God who exists in three distinct persons: the Father, the Son, and the Holy Spirit.

For there are three that bear record in heaven, the Father, the Word, and the Holy Ghost: and these three are one. (1 Jn. 5:7)

Jesus Christ is called "the Word" because He reveals and declares the Father. The Holy Spirit inspired the written word of God (2 Tim. 3:16) that we might know the Son of God.

**(1) In the beginning was the Word, and the Word was with God, and the Word was God.
(2) The same was in the beginning with God.
(3) All things were made by him; and without him was not any thing made that was made.** (Jn. 1:1-3)

(14) And the Word was made flesh, and dwelt among us, (and we beheld his glory, the glory as of the only begotten of the Father,) full of grace and truth.
(18) No man hath seen God at any time; the only begotten Son, which is in the bosom of the Father, he hath declared *him*. (Jn. 1:14, 18)

Search the scriptures; for in them ye think ye have eternal life: and they are they which testify of me. (Jn. 5:39)

(13) Howbeit when he, the Spirit of truth, is come, he will guide you into all truth: for he shall not speak of himself; but whatsoever he shall hear, *that* shall he speak: and he will shew you things to come.
(14) He shall glorify me: for he shall receive of mine, and shall shew *it* unto you. (Jn. 16:13-14)

What it Means to Know God

We are not talking about merely knowing things about God based on what others have told us. We are talking about the Spirit of God giving us spiritual knowledge of God through personal faith in His word. Upon salvation we know God as our Saviour, but believers need to increase in the knowledge of who He is and all that He has done for us.

The apostle Paul prayed for saved people to grow in the knowledge of God.

(15) Wherefore I also, after I heard of your faith in the Lord Jesus, and love unto all the saints,

**(16) Cease not to give thanks for you, making mention of you in my prayers;
(17) That the God of our Lord Jesus Christ, the Father of glory, may give unto you the spirit of wisdom and revelation in the knowledge of him:** (Eph 1:15-17)

**(9) For this cause we also, since the day we heard *it,* do not cease to pray for you, and to desire that ye might be filled with the knowledge of his will in all wisdom and spiritual understanding;
(10) That ye might walk worthy of the Lord unto all pleasing, being fruitful in every good work, and increasing in the knowledge of God;** (Col. 1:9-10)

In another prayer, Paul prayed that we know the love of Christ that passes knowledge. How can we know something that passes knowledge? It passes human knowledge, but we may know it by the Spirit of God (1 Cor. 2:11).

And to know the love of Christ, which passeth knowledge, that ye might be filled with all the fulness of God.
(Eph 3:19)

The Importance of Knowing God

There is nothing more important than having a true knowledge of God. How can we trust, worship, walk with, and serve a God that we do not know?

Lacking in the knowledge of God has a detrimental effect on our life.

My people are destroyed for lack of knowledge: (Hos. 4:6a)

(33) Be not deceived: evil communications corrupt good manners.
(34) Awake to righteousness, and sin not; for some have not the knowledge of God: I speak *this* to your shame.
(1 Cor. 15:33-34)

On the other hand, growing in the knowledge of God will have a wonderful effect on our life. We will trust God to the degree we know how good, loving, wise, and faithful He is. The more we know how holy, righteous, and powerful God is, the more we will desire to worship Him. Knowing that God is light, we should walk with Him by faith in the light of His word (Ps. 119:105). If we know the mercies of God, we will consider presenting our bodies a living sacrifice to be our reasonable service (Rom. 12:1).

(23) Thus saith the LORD, Let not the wise *man* glory in his wisdom, neither let the mighty *man* glory in his might, let not the rich *man* glory in his riches:
(24) But let him that glorieth glory in this, that he understandeth and knoweth me, that I *am* the LORD which exercise lovingkindness, judgment, and righteousness, in the earth: for in these *things* I delight, saith the LORD. (Jer. 9:23-24)

How to Find the Knowledge of God

God has PARTIALLY revealed Himself to everyone through conscience and creation.

**(19) Because that which may be known of God is manifest in them; for God hath shewed *it* unto them.
(20) For the invisible things of him from the creation of the world are clearly seen, being understood by the things that are made, *even* his eternal power and Godhead; so that they are without excuse:** (Rom. 1:19-20)

**(1) The heavens declare the glory of God; and the firmament sheweth his handywork.
(2) Day unto day uttereth speech, and night unto night sheweth knowledge.
(3) *There is* no speech nor language, *where* their voice is not heard.
(4) Their line is gone out through all the earth, and their words to the end of the world. In them hath he set a tabernacle for the sun,
(5) Which *is* as a bridegroom coming out of his chamber, *and* rejoiceth as a strong man to run a race.
(6) His going forth *is* from the end of the heaven, and his circuit unto the ends of it: and there is nothing hid from the heat thereof.** (Ps. 19:1-6)

By the witness of creation, we know that God is all-powerful for only an all-powerful God could create this universe. Only a fool would say there is no God (Ps. 14:1; 53:1). By the witness of our conscience, we know that God is a moral God because there are moral laws written upon our hearts.

God has PERFECTLY revealed Himself to His people through His word.

(7) The law of the LORD *is* perfect, converting the soul: the testimony of the LORD *is* sure, making wise the simple.
(8) The statutes of the LORD *are* right, rejoicing the heart: the commandment of the LORD *is* pure, enlightening the eyes.
(9) The fear of the LORD *is* clean, enduring for ever: the judgments of the LORD *are* true *and* righteous altogether.
(10) More to be desired *are they* than gold, yea, than much fine gold: sweeter also than honey and the honeycomb. (Ps. 19:7-10)

We will not find the true knowledge of God in our own thoughts, feelings, or experiences. It is only found in the pages of His word. The Bible is not everything God knows, but it contains everything we need to know about God and His purpose and plan for the ages. We will never learn it all in a lifetime of study.

That I may know him, and the power of his resurrection, and the fellowship of his sufferings, being made conformable unto his death; (Phil. 3:10)

When the apostle Paul said, "That I may know him" he had been saved for many years, saw the Lord several times (he was an apostle, we will not see the Lord until we get to Heaven), and he had received an abundance of revelations from Him. He had also been caught up into the third heaven (2 Cor. 12:1-7). This tells us that growing in the knowledge of God is a lifelong pursuit.

Like anything that is worth pursuing, we must put effort into knowing God by studying His word.

Study to shew thyself approved unto God, a workman that needeth not to be ashamed, rightly dividing the word of truth. (2 Tim. 2:15)

In the passage below there are seven steps to finding the knowledge of God.

(1) My son, if thou wilt <u>receive my words</u>, and <u>hide my commandments with thee</u>;
(2) So that thou <u>incline thine ear unto wisdom</u>, *and* <u>apply thine heart to understanding</u>;
(3) Yea, if thou <u>criest after knowledge</u>, *and* <u>liftest up thy voice for understanding</u>;
(4) If thou <u>seekest her as silver, and searchest for her as *for* hid treasures</u>;
(5) Then shalt thou understand the fear of the LORD, and find the knowledge of God.
(6) For the LORD giveth wisdom: out of his mouth *cometh* knowledge and understanding. (Prov. 2:1-6)

Chapter 2
Review Questions

1. What is the purpose of salvation?

2. Who are the three persons of the Godhead?
    1) _____
    2) _____
    3) _____

3. What kind of knowledge should we have of God?

4. Why is the knowledge of God important?

5. Where do we find the knowledge of God?

Chapter 3
The Bible

As we learned in the last chapter, we know God through His word and not through our own thoughts, feelings, and experiences. We cannot overemphasize the importance of the Bible in our Christian life!

The word "Bible" is derived from the Greek word *biblios* which means "a book." The Bible is not just a book: it is God's Book!

Seek ye out of the book of the LORD, and read: (Isa. 34:16a)

This verse tells us that God wrote a book and it is available. Therefore, we should read it.

The Bible has a number of titles, such as "the scriptures" and "the word of God."

And beginning at Moses and all the prophets, he expounded unto them in all the scriptures the things concerning himself. (Lk. 24:27)

So then faith *cometh* by hearing, and hearing by the word of God. (Rom. 10:17)

The Importance of the Bible

We will understand the importance of the Bible when we consider the value that God places upon it.

1) God has magnified His word above all His name (Ps. 138:2).
2) God said that man must live by His word (Matt. 4:4).
3) God gave His word some of the same titles and attributes as He does Himself.

For example:
- The Bible – **Holding forth <u>the word of life</u>** (Phil. 2:16a)
  Christ – **That which was from the beginning, which we have heard, which we have seen with our eyes, which we have looked upon, and our hands have handled, of <u>the Word of life</u>;** (1 Jn. 1:1)

- The Bible – **For the word of God *is* quick, and powerful, and sharper than any twoedged sword, piercing even to the dividing asunder of soul and spirit, and of the joints and marrow, and *is* <u>a discerner of the thoughts and intents of the heart</u>.** (Heb. 4:12)
  Christ – **And Jesus knowing their thoughts said, Wherefore think ye evil in your hearts?** (Matt. 9:4)

How important is the Bible in the life of a Christian? Without God's word we could not:
1) Be saved (Eph. 1:13)
2) Grow spiritually (1 Pet. 2:2)
3) Know God's will (Col. 1:9)
4) Live a sanctified life (Jn. 17:17; Eph. 5:26)
5) Worship God (Jn. 4:24)

6) Serve God (Phil. 2:16)
7) Defeat temptation (1 Cor. 10:13)
8) War a good warfare (Eph. 6:17)
9) Please God (Heb. 11:6)

How God Gave us the Bible

The Bible is one book that consists of 66 books. There are 39 books in the Old Testament and 27 books in the New Testament. These books were written over a period of about 1,500 years by about 40 different writers and yet they come together as ONE perfect Book without error or contradiction. Think about how amazing that is. If 40 different writers wrote 66 books on medicine over a period of 1,500 years, it would be a confusing mess. The explanation for the Bible's perfection is that God Himself is its Author. The Bible has one central figure: the Lord Jesus Christ.

How God gave us His word:
- **Inspiration** (2 Tim. 3:16) – Inspiration is the process by which the Spirit of God gives the words of scripture. The words of scripture are "spirit and life" (Jn. 6:63) which means the Bible is a living Book (Phil. 2:16; Heb. 4:12).
- **Preservation** (Ps. 12:6-7) – Preservation is the process by which God ensures that His words are kept pure and continue to exist on the earth. The original writings of the 66 books have all perished but the copies are just as pure. God used Israel to preserve the Old Testament and the Church to preserve the New Testament.

The Old Testament was originally written in Hebrew and the New Testament in Greek. The King James Bible is the word of

God in English. Some will insist that translation mars the original words. However, God invented languages and is capable of ensuring that His Book is not marred in translation.

In the English language there are hundreds of versions of the Bible. Only one of them is perfect: the King James Bible. The others are based on corrupt manuscripts and have words that are omitted, added, and changed. For example, the modern versions omit the vital words "through his blood" in Colossians 1:14 (see Study Notes on the King James Bible for many other examples). Satan attacks the word of God (Gen. 3:1-5). God is not the "author of confusion" (1 Cor. 14:33). Therefore, it is Satan and not God that is behind the hundreds of different versions of the Bible in English.

Why God Gave us the Bible

(16) All scripture *is* given by inspiration of God, and *is* profitable for doctrine, for reproof, for correction, for instruction in righteousness:
(17) That the man of God may be perfect, throughly furnished unto all good works. (2 Tim. 3:16-17)

In the above passage, the apostle Paul not only tells us that the scripture is given by inspiration of God, but he also tells us why God gave us the scripture.

1) Doctrine – teaching that is right.
2) Reproof – what is not right.
3) Correction – how to get right.
4) Instruction – how to stay right.

The believer who receives doctrine, reproof, correction, and instruction from the scripture will grow to be "perfect" (not sinless but spiritually strong and mature).

It is important to note that this passage is given in the context of what will be happening in the "last days" (2 Tim. 3:1) before Christ comes for us. We are certainly in those days. One of the main marks of the "last days" is religious DECEPTION (2 Tim. 3:13). Believing the Bible is our safeguard against deception.

The Bible is our final authority in all matters of faith and practice. God's written word is "more sure" than a supernatural vision or hearing a voice from heaven.

(16) For we have not followed cunningly devised fables, when we made known unto you the power and coming of our Lord Jesus Christ, but were eyewitnesses of his majesty.
(17) For he received from God the Father honour and glory, when there came such a voice to him from the excellent glory, This is my beloved Son, in whom I am well pleased.
(18) And this voice which came from heaven we heard, when we were with him in the holy mount.
(19) We have also <u>a more sure word</u> of prophecy; whereunto ye do well that ye take heed, as unto a light that shineth in a dark place, until the day dawn, and the day star arise in your hearts:
(20) Knowing this first, that no prophecy of the scripture is of any private interpretation.

(21) For the prophecy came not in old time by the will of man: but holy men of God spake *as they were* moved by the Holy Ghost. (2 Pet. 1:16-21)

The desire that some people have for signs more than the scripture is a mark of immaturity and not spirituality. In the Bible, God uses signs in His dealings with the nation of Israel (1 Cor. 1:22). The apostle Paul clearly said that signs would cease (1 Cor. 13:8-13), and they have. God will not give us signs and visions today. We have the perfect word of God and that is all we need. Satan can use signs to deceive (2 Cor. 11:13-14) but the word of God is absolute truth and is therefore "more sure."

The Key to Understanding the Bible

In the same epistle that Paul said, "All scripture is given by inspiration of God, and is profitable," he also told us how to study it (2 Tim. 2:15). That the Bible must be rightly divided means that while all scripture is for us, it was not all written directly to us. The whole Bible is the truth, but there are divisions that God put in His word. What was truth for the nation of Israel under the law may not be truth for the Body of Christ under grace (Rom. 6:14).

For example, God gave the Sabbath as a sign between Himself and Israel. The weekly Sabbath is Saturday (the seventh day of the week), and it has never been changed to Sunday (which is the first day of the week). The Body of Christ is not commanded to keep the Sabbath. We assemble on Sunday because it was the day Christ rose from the dead (Matt. 28:1-8; Acts 20:7).

Doctrine given TO Israel:
(12) And the LORD spake unto Moses, saying,
(13) Speak thou also unto the children of Israel, saying, Verily my sabbaths ye shall keep: for it *is* a sign between me and you throughout your generations; that *ye* may know that I *am* the LORD that doth sanctify you.
(14) Ye shall keep the sabbath therefore; for it *is* holy unto you: every one that defileth it shall surely be put to death: for whosoever doeth *any* work therein, that soul shall be cut off from among his people. (Ex. 31:12-14)

Doctrine TO the Body of Christ:
Let no man therefore judge you in meat, or in drink, or in respect of an holyday, or of the new moon, or of the sabbath *days:* (Col. 2:16)

Satan is a deceiver, and he will use the Bible to deceive people by taking it out of context.

What to Do with the Bible

It is a great privilege to have a copy of the pure word of God. With great privilege comes great responsibility.

1) **Believe** (Ps. 119:128) – Believing God's word is faith (Rom. 10:17) and without faith it is impossible to please Him (Heb. 11:6). The Holy Spirit that gave us the words of the Bible must be our teacher and guide if we are going to understand it. If we do not truly believe His words, He will not open our understanding to them.
2) **Read** (1 Tim. 4:13) – Simply reading the Bible is where we must begin. We recommend that you begin by

reading the thirteen epistles of the apostle Paul (Romans through Philemon), and then start in Genesis and read through the Bible. By reading four chapters each day, you will read the entire Bible in a year.

3) **Study** (2 Tim. 2:15) – Studying the Bible is more intense than just reading it. We must examine it carefully with the purpose of understanding what it says.

4) **Meditate** (1 Tim. 4:15) – To meditate on the word of God is to think deeply upon the truth we have learned through personal Bible study. We will not be "nourished up in the words of faith and of good doctrine" (1 Tim. 4:6) without meditating on what we are learning as we study God's word. Meditation is to the spirit what digestion is to the body.

5) **Hide it in our heart** (Ps. 119:11; Col. 3:16) – As we meditate on the truth, it will dwell in our heart.

6) **Apply** (1 Tim. 4:6-7) – Learning the Bible should have a personal impact on our lives.

7) **Obey** (Rom. 6:17) – There is doctrine in the Bible that we must not only learn, but also obey.

8) **Teach** (2 Tim. 2:2) – We must pass on the truth we have learned to others. If we cannot communicate what we have learned, we have not truly learned it.

Basic Bible Truth

Chapter 3
Review Questions

1. God has magnified _____ above all His name.

2. Name three reasons the Bible is important to our Christian life.
   1) _____
   2) _____
   3) _____

3. God gave us His word by _____ and we have it today because of _____.

4. Which is English Bible is the pure word of God?

5. What is the key to understanding the Bible?

6. Name three things we are to do with the Bible.
   1) _____
   2) _____
   3) _____

Chapter 4
Following Christ Through Paul

One of the first things a new believer should learn is that the apostle Paul was chosen by Christ to be the pattern and spokesman (i.e., Christ spoke through him, 2 Cor. 13:3) for the church to follow today.

(16) Wherefore I beseech you, be ye followers of me.
(17) For this cause have I sent unto you Timotheus, who is my beloved son, and faithful in the Lord, who shall bring you into remembrance of <u>my ways which be in Christ</u>, as I teach every where in every church.
(1 Cor. 4:16-17)

Be ye followers of me, even <u>as I also am of Christ</u>.
(1 Cor. 11:1)

(15) This *is* a faithful saying, and worthy of all acceptation, that Christ Jesus came into the world to save sinners; of whom I am chief.
(16) Howbeit for this cause I obtained mercy, <u>that in me first Jesus Christ might shew forth all longsuffering, for a pattern</u> to them which should hereafter believe on him to life everlasting. (1 Tim. 1:15)

During His ministry on earth, Christ chose and sent twelve apostles to the twelve tribes of Israel (Matt. 19:28). After Israel fell as a nation (they will be saved in the future, Rom. 11:25-27),

Christ from Heaven chose and sent Paul to be the apostle of the Gentiles. If we are going to follow Christ, we must do so by receiving the one He sent to show us how to do so.

Verily, verily, I say unto you, He that receiveth whomsoever I send receiveth me; and he that receiveth me receiveth him that sent me. (Jn. 13:20)

And he said unto me, Depart: for I will send thee far hence unto the Gentiles. (Acts 22:21)

For I speak to you Gentiles, inasmuch as I am the apostle of the Gentiles, I magnify mine office: (Rom 11:13)

Sadly, very few churches today recognize this truth. This is nothing new for they were turning away from following Paul during his ministry.

This thou knowest, that all they which are in Asia be turned away from me; of whom are Phygellus and Hermogenes. (2 Tim. 1:15)

In saying that we are to follow Paul, we are simply quoting scripture. We are not exalting a man or making more out of Paul than the scripture does. We are certainly not putting Christ and Paul on the same level. We know that Paul was the "chief of sinners" saved by grace, while Christ is the sinless Son of God and the Saviour of sinners. We know that Paul was nothing in himself while Christ is everything for "in him dwelleth all the fulness of the Godhead bodily" (Col. 2:9). But it was to Paul that the glorified Lord committed the revelation of His message and program for this present age.

In the same way that God made Moses His spokesman to Israel, He made Paul His spokesman to the Body of Christ.

It is not the person but the office of Paul that is to be magnified (Rom. 11:13). Paul rebuked the carnal Corinthians for following him as a man (1 Cor. 1:10-17). We are to follow the DOCTRINE that Christ revealed through Paul (1 Tim. 1:3; 6:3; 2 Tim. 1:13; 2:2; 3:10-14).

Even though the word of God plainly tells believers in this present age to follow the apostle Paul, many professing Christians resent that idea when presented with it and claim to follow the whole Bible instead. However, that is not possible because God's word has some different things to say to different people living under different dispensations.

Dispensation (1 Cor. 9:17; Eph. 1:10; 3:2; Col. 1:25) – A dispensing of divine revelation. A way in which God deals with man.

God does not change in His person, principles, or promises (Mal. 3:6; Heb. 13:8), but He certainly does change in His dealings with man. If you do not recognize this fact, the Bible will be a confusing book to you. We cannot possibly obey all the instructions found within its pages because there are different instructions given concerning some of the same issues.

Consider the basic issue of what we are to eat:
1) Adam (Gen. 1:29) – no meat
2) Noah (Gen. 9:3-4) – meat without blood
3) Moses (Lev. 11:46-47) – only "clean" meats
4) Paul (1 Tim. 4:1-5) – nothing is to be refused

There is a difference between moral truth and dispensational truth. There are moral principles that never change from age to age. For example, murder is always a sin. As we saw in the last chapter, the sabbath day is an example of dispensational truth. God gave Israel sabbaths to observe, but He never gave them to the Body of Christ (Col. 2:16). The moral truth of the law still applies today. The apostle Paul reaffirmed nine of the ten commandments (Rom. 13:8-10).

All of the Bible is the word of God and is therefore profitable FOR us, but it is not all written directly TO us. We need to read and study the whole Bible. When we come across something that does not line up with what the apostle Paul taught in his epistles, we are to follow what Christ said through Paul directly to us in this present age.

Consider what I say; and the Lord give thee understanding in all things. (2 Tim. 2:7)

We are not pitting the words of Moses, Jesus Christ, or Peter against Paul. All scripture is given by inspiration of God and is therefore the word of God (2 Tim. 3:16). But the word of God must be rightly divided if it is going to be understood. All scripture is profitable for us, but we will not gain the profit that God has for us in His word unless we study it His way.

Study to shew thyself approved unto God, a workman that needeth not to be ashamed, rightly dividing the word of truth. (2 Tim. 2:15)

Note three things in this key verse:
    1) The Mandate – What we are to do – "Study"

2) The Motive – Why we are to do it – "to shew thyself approved unto God"
3) The Method – How we are to do it – "rightly dividing the word of truth"

Rightly dividing the word of truth is not an issue of dividing truth from error because there are no errors in the Bible. It is an issue of recognizing and consistently maintaining the divisions that God put in His word. What was truth for Israel under the law may not be truth for the Body of Christ under grace. This is the dispensational approach to Bible study.

Chapter 4
Review Questions

1. The apostle Paul was chosen by Christ to be the _____ and _____ for us to follow today.

2. It is not the person but the _____ of Paul that is to be magnified.

3. What is a dispensation?

4. All of the Bible is _____ us but it is not all written ___ us.

5. The key verse for Bible study (2 Tim. 2:15) tells us:
   1) What to do _____
   2) Why to do it _____
   3) How to do it _____

Chapter 5
Prayer

In the last chapter we learned from the scripture that the Lord raised up the apostle Paul to be the example for believers to follow today.

Those things, which ye have both learned, and received, and heard, and seen in me, do: and the God of peace shall be with you. (Phil. 4:9)

Paul was a man of prayer. Throughout his epistles we find him constantly praying and requesting prayer. In this lesson we will answer basic questions about prayer.

What is Prayer?

Prayer is simply talking to God. It is an expression of dependence upon God and should naturally flow out of our relationship with Him.

And he *(Jesus Christ)* **said, Abba, Father, all things *are* possible unto thee; take away this cup from me: nevertheless not what I will, but what thou wilt.** (Mk. 14:36)

And because ye are sons, God hath sent forth the Spirit of his Son into your hearts, crying, Abba, Father. (Gal. 4:6)

The Aramaic word, "Abba" expresses a close relationship, like our English word, "Daddy." Because we are in Christ, we have this relationship with the Father.

All believers have the same relationship with God but not all believers cultivate and enjoy that relationship. Communication is crucial to a healthy relationship. Bible study and prayer go hand in hand. The Bible is how God talks to us and prayer is how we talk to Him.

What a great privilege that we have full and free access to God!

For through <u>him</u> *(Christ)* we both have access by one <u>Spirit</u> unto the <u>Father</u>. (Eph. 2:18)

We pray:
1) To the Father (Eph. 3:14-15) – We are His children (Gal. 3:26).
2) In the name of the Son (Eph. 5:20) – We have access through Christ (Eph. 3:12).
3) In the Spirit (Eph. 6:18) – Paul is not referring to a "prayer language" or emotional experience. All believers are in the Spirit (Rom. 8:9, 14-15).

How Do We Pray?

Prayer is a spiritual exercise and therefore the physical posture, place, and time are not the issue. We may pray anywhere and at any time. It is good to spend dedicated time with God, but we are to pray without ceasing (1 Thess. 5:17), meaning that we should pray throughout the day as the need arises. We can pray without saying words because God knows our heart.

Prayer should be a top priority (1 Tim. 2:1) and something in which we are instant (i.e., ready, Rom. 12:12), continuing (Col. 4:2), watching, and persevering (Eph. 6:18).

Prayer should involve:
1) Praise
2) Thanksgiving (Phil. 4:6)
3) Confession of sins – for repentance (2 Cor. 7:10), not forgiveness because we are already forgiven (Col. 2:13)
4) Intercession – praying for others
5) Supplication – asking God to supply a need

The main thing is that prayer must be offered in **faith** based an intelligent understanding of **God's will** as revealed in His word (1 Cor. 14:15; 2 Tim. 2:15). Our prayers need to be in line with what God is doing because we will never convince Him to do otherwise. Prayer is not about getting God to do our will but submitting to His.

Not every prayer promise in the Bible was given to us. You will become frustrated and defeated in prayer if you claim promises that God did not give you. For example, Christ gave the twelve apostles, who will sit on twelve thrones in the kingdom (Matt. 19:28), a prayer promise that did not work in the life of the apostle Paul.

And all things, whatsoever ye shall ask in prayer, believing, ye shall receive. (Matt. 21:22)

(7) And lest I should be exalted above measure through the abundance of the revelations, there was given to me a

thorn in the flesh, the messenger of Satan to buffet me, lest I should be exalted above measure.
(8) For this thing I besought the Lord thrice, that it might depart from me.
(9) And he said unto me, My grace is sufficient for thee: for my strength is made perfect in weakness. Most gladly therefore will I rather glory in my infirmities, that the power of Christ may rest upon me. (2 Cor. 12:7-9)

God did not promise to always give us whatever we ask for, but He will give us His peace if we trust Him.

(6) Be careful for nothing; but in every thing by prayer and supplication with thanksgiving let your requests be made known unto God.
(7) And the peace of God, which passeth all understanding, shall keep your hearts and minds through Christ Jesus. (Phil. 4:6-7)

What Should We Pray About?

We are free to pray about whatever is on our hearts. Of course, spiritual things should be the priority in prayer because they are what is most important (1 Tim. 2:1-4). Paul is our example, and his prayers primarily concerned spiritual things.

We should be praying for souls to be saved (Rom. 10:1) and for saints to be edified in the faith (Col. 4:12). We should pray for those who preach the truth of God's word rightly divided (Eph. 6:18-20; Col. 4:2-4).

Study Notes

Should we pray about physical, and material needs? Paul prayed about his thorn in the flesh. God may not give us what we ask, but He will give us grace and peace as we trust Him. There is no promise of healing as God gave Israel (Jam. 1:1; 5:14-15), but that does not mean God will not have mercy on us as He did for Epaphroditus (Phil. 2:25-27). It is possible, but not a guarantee.

Should we pray for God's guidance in our lives? We should seek guidance through the word of God as we talk to Him about it (Prov. 3:5-6).

(5) Now I will come unto you, when I shall pass through Macedonia: for I do pass through Macedonia.
(6) And it may be that I will abide, yea, and winter with you, that ye may bring me on my journey whithersoever I go.
(7) For I will not see you now by the way; but I trust to tarry a while with you, <u>if the Lord permit</u>.
(8) But I will tarry at Ephesus until Pentecost.
(9) For a <u>great door and effectual is opened unto me</u>, and *there are* many adversaries. (1 Cor. 16:5-9)

Does Prayer Make a Difference?

Paul was always praying and requesting prayer because he knew it made a difference.

Ye also helping together by prayer for us, that for the gift *bestowed* upon us by the means of many persons thanks may be given by many on our behalf. (2 Cor. 1:11)

But withal prepare me also a lodging: for I trust that through your prayers I shall be given unto you. (Phile. 22)

As limited human beings we do not know what to pray for as we ought. Thankfully, the Spirit makes intercession for us according to the will of God.

(26) Likewise the Spirit also helpeth our infirmities: for we know not what we should pray for as we ought: but the Spirit itself maketh intercession for us with groanings which cannot be uttered.
(27) And he that searcheth the hearts knoweth what *is* the mind of the Spirit, because he maketh intercession for the saints according to *the will of* God.
(28) And we know that all things work together for good to them that love God, to them who are the called according to *his* purpose. (Rom. 8:26-28)

Chapter 5
Review Questions

1. Prayer is simply _____.

2. Name three things prayer should include.
    1) _____
    2) _____
    3) _____

3. The main thing is that prayer must be offered in _____ and based on an intelligent understanding of _____ as revealed in His _____.

4. Were all of the prayer promises in the Bible given to us?

5. What kind of things should be the priority in our prayers?

Chapter 6
The Church

The words "church" and "churches" are found 114 times in the King James Bible. The church should be important to us because it is important to the Lord.

**(25) Husbands, love your wives, even as Christ also loved the church, and gave himself for it;
(26) That he might sanctify and cleanse it with the washing of water by the word,
(27) That he might present it to himself a glorious church, not having spot, or wrinkle, or any such thing; but that it should be holy and without blemish.** (Eph. 5:25-27)

What is a Church?

A church is an assembly of people called out for a specific purpose, the nature and purpose of which must be determined by the context. In the Bible, a church is a called-out assembly of God's people. It is a misuse of the term to use it regarding a building or denomination.

Whatever God does, Satan seeks to corrupt and counterfeit it. Therefore, we know that there is false doctrine about the church and there are false churches (2 Cor. 11:3-4, 13-15).

How can we discern sound doctrine from false doctrine? How can we discern a true church from a false church? We must not look to the traditions and teachings of men, but we must look to the word of God.

Different Churches in the Bible

It is important to understand that there are different churches in the Bible. There are churches that differ in their calling, purpose, doctrine, and destiny. Failure to rightly divide these churches leads to confusion.

This is he, that was in the church in the wilderness with the angel which spake to him in the mount Sina, and *with* our fathers: who received the lively oracles to give unto us: (Acts 7:38)

Israel was called out of Egypt and assembled in the wilderness as God's chosen nation. This church was a literal nation of people that God set apart from the Gentiles and brought under the covenant of law. This is not the church that God is building today. The word "church" is not used in the OT because it is a word translated from Greek and not Hebrew. However, when we compare the following two verses, we learn that the OT word translated "congregation" is related to the NT word translated "church."

I will declare thy name unto my brethren: in the midst of the <u>congregation</u> will I praise thee. (Ps. 22:22)

Saying, I will declare thy name unto my brethren, in the midst of the <u>church</u> will I sing praise unto thee. (Heb. 2:12)

Comparing these verses also proves there are different churches in the Bible because there is a church that was PROPHESIED in the OT. The church which God is building in this present age was a mystery (or secret) that was hid in God until Christ from heaven revealed it to the apostle Paul (Eph. 3:1-12).

(24) Who now rejoice in my sufferings for you, and fill up that which is behind of the afflictions of Christ in my flesh for his body's sake, which is the church:
(25) Whereof I am made a minister, according to the dispensation of God which is given to me for you, to fulfil the word of God;
(26) *Even* the mystery which hath been hid from ages and from generations, but now is made manifest to his saints: (Col. 1:24-26)

Two Churches Today

There are two churches you should be a member of in this present age. There is one spiritual church that we become a member of upon **salvation**. There are local and visible churches through which believers **serve** the Lord. The Body of Christ is a spiritual organism made up regenerated members. The local church is a visible organization made up of professing believers.

1. **The Body of Christ**

This church is made up of all believers that are called out of the world by believing the gospel of the grace of God (2 Thess. 2:14) and are assembled together in one spiritual Body in which there is neither Jew nor Gentile. The moment a sinner trusts Christ as Saviour the Holy Spirit baptizes him into the Body of Christ. The Lord Jesus Christ is the Head of the church and all saved people in this present age are members of it.

(27) For as many of you as have been baptized into Christ have put on Christ.

(28) There is neither Jew nor Greek, there is neither bond nor free, there is neither male nor female: for ye are all one in Christ Jesus. (Gal. 3:27-28)

(12) For as the body is one, and hath many members, and all the members of that one body, being many, are one body: so also *is* Christ.
(13) For by one Spirit are we all baptized into one body, whether *we be* Jews or Gentiles, whether *we be* bond or free; and have been all made to drink into one Spirit.
(1 Cor. 12:12-13)

(4) But God, who is rich in mercy, for his great love wherewith he loved us,
(5) Even when we were dead in sins, hath quickened us together with Christ, (by grace ye are saved;)
(6) And hath raised *us* up together, and made *us* sit together in heavenly *places* in Christ Jesus: (Eph. 2:4-6)

The fact that this church was a mystery hidden from the OT prophets and that in it there is neither "Jew nor Greek" proves that it is a different church from the ones mentioned before the ministry of the apostle Paul.

2. The Local Church

The majority of times the word "church" is used In the Bible it is in reference to a local church. The apostle Paul started local churches and wrote letters to them by inspiration of God. It is the will of God for believers to assemble in local churches for the ministry of the word and to labor together to get the gospel to the lost. The local church is to be organized according to the order set forth in Paul's epistles (1 Cor. 14:40; Titus 1:5).

What to Look for in a Church

The local church is to be the pillar and ground of the truth in a community. It is a visible manifestation of the invisible Body of Christ.

(14) These things write I unto thee, hoping to come unto thee shortly:
(15) But if I tarry long, that thou mayest know how thou oughtest to behave thyself in the house of God, which is the church of the living God, the pillar and ground of the truth. (1 Tim. 3:14-15)

The important things to look for in a church are not programs, activities, and music. It is sound doctrine and the sincere desire to walk in it and share it with others.

The main questions you should ask when looking for a church are:
1) Do you believe the King James Bible is the inspired and preserved word of God?
2) What is the gospel of our salvation?
3) Do you preach and teach the Bible rightly divided?
4) May I have a copy of your doctrinal statement?
5) What is the purpose of the ministry?

Sadly, most "churches" today are nothing more than worldly social clubs teaching the philosophies and traditions of men. For those who do not have a Bible-believing church in their area, we recommend that they study the Bible at home and take advantage of the sound Bible preaching and teaching that is available online. If you are being edified through the online ministry of a local church, you should support it through prayer and giving. Perhaps the Lord could use you one day to help get a good church started in your area.

There may be a church in your area that you do not agree with on everything, but they believe the Bible, preach salvation by grace, study the Bible dispensationally, and they are headed in the right direction. Perhaps you could be a blessing to them. Remember, church should be about serving, not being served.

Why Go to Church?

We should not go to church out of religious ritual or with selfish motives. Going to church with the right motives will help us to be faithful and to get more out of it.

1. **Relationships**
   - *Serving God* – We are in Christ, and He is in us. We don't have to go to church in order to worship God. We are seated with Him in heavenly places (Eph. 2:6). We have full and free access to God. Yet, we know it is God's will that we assemble together with other believers. If we love Christ, we will love His church. What is important to Him should be important to us. God is pleased with the corporate worship of believers who are endeavoring to keep the unity of the Spirit in the bond of peace (Eph. 4:3). We should assemble together to serve God and be edified in His word. A church must put the Lord before people. We assemble first and foremost for His glory.
   - *Serving one another* – We are not only members of Christ, but we are members of one another (1 Cor. 12:12-27). We are in the same spiritual family (1 Tim. 5:1-2). There should be a warm and loving atmosphere among God's people.

2. Responsibilities

With great privilege and blessing comes responsibility. Going to church is not just about sitting around and enjoying each other's company. God has given us a work to do. Yet most people that go to church have the attitude, "What are you going to do for me?" We are to be servants, faithfully serving God and one another. There is something for everybody to do.

- Edification (Eph. 4:12-16) – Build up one another in the faith by the word of God.
- Evangelism (1 Thess. 1:8)
- Bearing one another's burdens (Gal. 6:2)
- Giving (Gal. 6:6-10) – We should all have a part in supporting our local church and the cause of world missions. We are not under the law of tithing, but we are to be grace givers (2 Cor. 9:6-8). Why would believers under grace give LESS to support the Lord's work than Israel was required to do under the law? Paul had much to say about giving (Acts 20:35; Rom. 15:26-28; 1 Cor. 9:1-14; 16:1-2; 2 Cor. 8-9; Gal. 2:10; 6:6-10; Eph. 4:28; Phil. 4:10-19; 1 Tim. 5:17-18; Titus 3:13-14). If every member gave cheerfully according to what they have, it would make a difference and meet the need.
- Praying with and for one another (Col. 4:12; 1 Tim. 2:1-4)
- Comforting one another (1 Thess. 5:11)

The local church is a family of believers. Do not merely attend church as a spectator. Be a faithful part of what God is doing in and through His people!

Study Notes

Chapter 6
Review Questions

1. What is a church?

2. Which verse proves there is more than one church in the Bible?

3. What two churches should we be members of today?
    1) _____
    2) _____

4. How do we become members of the Body of Christ?

5. What are the two main reasons we should go to church?
    1) _____
    2) _____

Chapter 7
The Believer's Two Natures

The word of God teaches that the believer has two natures. New believers must learn this doctrine as soon as possible lest they become confused, discouraged, and defeated.

Upon salvation we enjoy the "newness of life" that is in Christ. With a heart full of gratitude for salvation, and the price that Christ paid for that salvation, we desire to live as pure and right as possible. However, it does not take very long to realize that the fleshly desires are not gone, and that we are still tempted to commit the same sins we lived in before salvation. Without an understanding of what the Bible teaches concerning the two natures, the new believer will eventually lose the joy of salvation thinking that he cannot live the Christian life and may even doubt that he is saved.

The Explanation

One of the definitions for "nature" in Noah Webster's 1828 dictionary is, *"The essence, essential qualities or attributes of a thing, which constitute it what it is."*

How can one person have two natures? The Bible speaks of the corrupt nature of man (Eph. 2:3), and of the divine nature (2 Pet. 1:4).

That which is born of the flesh is flesh; and that which is born of the Spirit is spirit. (Jn. 3:6)

The flesh refers to human nature or what we are by physical birth. All born of the flesh are children of wrath and disobedience.

(1) And you *hath he quickened,* who were dead in trespasses and sins;
(2) Wherein in time past ye walked according to the course of this world, according to the prince of the power of the air, the spirit that now worketh in the children of disobedience:
(3) Among whom also we all had our conversation in times past in the lusts of our flesh, fulfilling the desires of the flesh and of the mind; and were by nature the children of wrath, even as others. (Eph. 2:1-3)

Let no man deceive you with vain words: for because of these things cometh the wrath of God upon the children of disobedience. (Eph. 5:6)

The first man, Adam, was created in the image of God and enjoyed fellowship with Him. However, Adam sinned against God and died spiritually, being separated from the Spirit of God. All that are born into this world are born in the image of Adam (Gen. 5:3). The law of nature is that kind begets kind. The flesh can only bring forth flesh.

There is a distinction between *sin* which is the root and *sins* which are the fruit. Sin dwells in our flesh (Rom. 7:17). No matter how religious a person may be, the flesh cannot be changed or improved. It's possible to make a "fair shew in the flesh" in regard to religion (Gal. 6:12).

Consider what the word of God says about the flesh:
1) It profits nothing (Jn. 6:63).
2) In it dwells no good thing (Rom. 7:18).
3) It is enmity against God and cannot please God (Rom. 8:7-8).
4) It cannot know the things of the Spirit of God (1 Cor. 2:14).
5) It is corrupt according to the deceitful lusts (Eph. 4:22).

Salvation is not reformation of the flesh but regeneration by the Spirit (Titus 3:3-7). To be born of the flesh is generation and to be born of the Spirit is regeneration. The regenerated believer has been "renewed in knowledge after the image of him that created him" (Col. 3:10). We are created in Christ Jesus unto good works (Eph. 2:10). We become members of the new creature, the church which is the Body of Christ (2 Cor. 5:17). We are taken out of the "old man," the flesh, by a SPIRITUAL circumcision and put into the "new man," the Body of Christ, by a SPIRITUAL baptism (Col. 2:10-12; 3:9-11).

The nature of the flesh is sin, but the nature of the Spirit is righteousness (Eph. 4:24). Both natures exist within the believer while we live on earth. The flesh cannot be changed and made good in the sight of God. The flesh will be with us until death, or until the Lord comes for us and we receive a new body.

The old nature and the new nature are opposite in:
- Origin – Flesh vs. Spirit
- Character – "works of the flesh" vs. "fruit of the Spirit"

- Destiny – Death vs. Life

The Conflict

The existence of two natures within the same person which are of contrary origin, character, and destiny causes a conflict.

(16) *This* I say then, Walk in the Spirit, and ye shall not fulfil the lust of the flesh.
(17) For the flesh lusteth against the Spirit, and the Spirit against the flesh: and these are contrary the one to the other: so that ye cannot do the things that ye would.
(Gal. 5:16-17)

The flesh desires to sin and the Spirit desires for us to be righteous. This is a conflict that every true believer will experience but it is one that many do not understand. One of the blessings of this conflict is the assurance it provides that we have been regenerated because a person that does not have the Spirit knows nothing of a conflict between the flesh and the Spirit.

Another blessing of this conflict is that it teaches us by experience that our flesh is totally corrupt and therefore we must depend on God for victory (Rom. 7:24-25; Phil. 3:3). We cannot live godly in the energy of the flesh. We know that we are a sinner when we get saved, but when the Spirit of God moves in, we begin to realize just how sinful the flesh really is! The light of the Spirit and the word of God makes this abundantly clear.

This conflict is no excuse to walk in defeat as a believer because we can "walk in the Spirit" and thereby not "fulfill the lust of the flesh."

We will not find victory in this conflict by putting ourselves under the law, which is a performance-based religious system (more on this in the next chapter). Trying to live under the law will only intensify this conflict and render us incapable of walking in victory over the flesh (1 Cor. 15:56; Gal. 5:17-18).

(14) For sin shall not have dominion over you: for ye are not under the law, but under grace.
(15) What then? shall we sin, because we are not under the law, but under grace? God forbid. (Rom 6:14-15)

The Victory

It is not our responsibility to defeat the flesh because Christ already defeated it for us. However, we have a responsibility to walk by faith in the victory Christ has given us.

Knowing this, that our old man is crucified with *him*, that the body of sin might be destroyed, that henceforth we should not serve sin. (Rom. 6:6)

In Romans 6 the apostle Paul teaches us how to enjoy the victory we have in Christ. That we have been spiritually baptized into Christ (Rom. 6:3-4) means that we are identified with Him in His death, burial, and resurrection. Verse 17 is the key verse in the chapter because it sums up the teaching of the whole passage in one verse. We have three parts to our being: spirit, soul, and body (1 Thess. 5:23).

But God be thanked, that ye were the servants of sin, but ye have <u>obeyed</u> from the <u>heart</u> that form of <u>doctrine</u> which was delivered you. (Rom. 6:17)

1) Doctrine (spirit) – **Know** that our old man is crucified with Christ (vv.1-10)
2) Heart (soul) – **Reckon** that we are dead to sin and alive unto God (v.11)
3) Obeyed (body) – **Yield** our members as instruments of righteousness (vv.12-23)

By faith we are to practically put off the old man and put on the new man in our daily walk (Eph. 4:17-32). We put off the conversation (i.e., manner of life) of the old man by walking in the Spirit (Gal. 5:17). All believers are in the Spirit (Rom. 8:9), but not all consistently walk in the Spirit (Gal. 5:25).

What does it mean to walk in the Spirit? It is not some kind of sensational experience accompanied by feelings and supernatural manifestations. We walk in the Spirit when we walk by faith in the word that He inspired and illuminates to our understanding.

By comparing the following two passages, we see the between being filled with the Spirit and the word of God.

(18) And be not drunk with wine, wherein is excess; but be filled with the Spirit;
(19) Speaking to yourselves in psalms and hymns and spiritual songs, singing and making melody in your heart to the Lord;
(20) Giving thanks always for all things unto God and the Father in the name of our Lord Jesus Christ;
(21) Submitting yourselves one to another in the fear of God. (Eph. 5:18-21)

Let the word of Christ dwell in you richly in all wisdom; teaching and admonishing one another in psalms and hymns and spiritual songs, singing with grace in your hearts to the Lord. (Col. 3:16)

We must feed the new man with the word of God (1 Pet. 2:2) and starve the old man by not making provision to fulfill the lusts if the flesh (Rom. 13:14). As in the physical realm, good spiritual health is based on proper nourishment and exercise.

(6) If thou put the brethren in remembrance of these things, thou shalt be a good minister of Jesus Christ, nourished up in the words of faith and of good doctrine, whereunto thou hast attained.
(7) But refuse profane and old wives' fables, and exercise thyself *rather* unto godliness.
(8) For bodily exercise profiteth little: but godliness is profitable unto all things, having promise of the life that now is, and of that which is to come. (1 Tim. 4:6-8)

Chapter 7
Review Questions

1. Salvation is not reformation of the _____ but regeneration by the _____. To be born of the _____ is generation and to be born of the _____ is regeneration.

2. The nature of the flesh is _____, but the nature of the Spirit is _____.

3. What is one of the blessings of the conflict we experience between the flesh and the Spirit?

4. What are the three key words in Romans 6 concerning how we can walk in victory over the flesh?
    1) _____
    2) _____
    3) _____

Chapter 8
Law and Grace

If we rightly divide the word of truth (2 Tim. 2:15), we will see the difference between God's dealings with Israel under the law and His dealings with the Body of Christ under grace.

For sin shall not have dominion over you: for ye are not under the law, but under grace. (Rom. 6:14)

It is vital that we understand the difference between law and grace because we cannot walk in the Spirit if we put ourselves under the law.

But if ye be led of the Spirit, ye are not under the law. (Gal. 5:18)

God has shown grace in every age (e.g., Gen. 6:8), but we are living in the Age of Grace in which He is showing grace to a greater degree than ever before.

(20) Moreover the law entered, that the offence might abound. But where sin abounded, grace did much more abound:
(21) That as sin hath reigned unto death, even so might grace reign through righteousness unto eternal life by Jesus Christ our Lord. (Rom. 5:20-21)

We are saved by grace, and we stand in grace (Rom 5:1-2). The moment we trust Christ as our Saviour, we are complete in Him

(Col. 2:10) and accepted in the beloved (Eph. 1:6). We cannot earn God's favor; we have it as a free gift through Jesus Christ.

The Difference Between Law and Grace

Under the law, God's blessings were based on the performance of His people. The language of the law is, "IF you obey, THEN you will be blessed."

(1) And it shall come to pass, if thou shalt hearken diligently unto the voice of the LORD thy God, to observe *and* to do all his commandments which I command thee this day, that the LORD thy God will set thee on high above all nations of the earth:
(2) And all these blessings shall come on thee, and overtake thee, if thou shalt hearken unto the voice of the LORD thy God.

(15) But it shall come to pass, if thou wilt not hearken unto the voice of the LORD thy God, to observe to do all his commandments and his statutes which I command thee this day; that all these curses shall come upon thee, and overtake thee: (Deut. 28:1-2, 15)

Under grace, God's blessings are freely given to us in the Lord Jesus Christ. Grace is the unmerited favor and kindness of God.

Blessed *be* the God and Father of our Lord Jesus Christ, who hath blessed us with all spiritual blessings in heavenly *places* in Christ: (Eph. 1:3)

Contrasts between law and grace:
  1) The law said, "Do and be blessed," but grace says, "You are blessed, now do."

2) The law required righteousness, but grace makes us righteous.
3) The law gave works for man to do, but grace gave words for man to believe.
4) The law cursed sinners, but grace justifies them.
5) The law is bondage to the flesh, but grace brings liberty in the Spirit.
6) The law results in death, but grace gives life.
7) The law was religion, but grace gives us a relationship.

Religion teaches that you must do certain works to either be saved and/or to stay right with God. Most churches are legalistic because they do not recognize Paul as the divinely appointed patten and spokesman for the Body of Christ. Paul's epistles are the most neglected books of the Bible in the average church today.

The book of Romans is the foundational book of doctrine for this age of grace and in it Paul systematically laid out the wonderful truth that we are justified and sanctified by faith without the deeds of the law. In Galatians he wrote to correct the legalism that was creeping into the churches of Galatia and showed plainly that we cannot mix law and grace. We are saved by grace, and we are to live our Christin life under grace.

In Romans and Galatians, the apostle Paul plainly declares that:
1) We are NOT JUSTIFIED by the law (Rom. 3:19-28; Gal. 2:16)
2) We are NOT UNDER the law in our walk (Rom. 6:14; Gal. 5:18)
3) We ARE DEAD to the law (Rom. 7:1-4; Gal. 2:19)
4) We ARE DELIVERED from the law (Rom. 7:5-6; Gal. 5:1)

Study Notes

The Problem with the Law

The law is holy, just, and good, but it cannot make sinners holy, just, and good.

(7) What shall we say then? *Is* the law sin? God forbid. Nay, I had not known sin, but by the law: for I had not known lust, except the law had said, Thou shalt not covet.
(8) But sin, taking occasion by the commandment, wrought in me all manner of concupiscence. For without the law sin *was* dead.
(9) For I was alive without the law once: but when the commandment came, sin revived, and I died.
(10) And the commandment, which *was ordained* to life, I found *to be* unto death.
(11) For sin, taking occasion by the commandment, deceived me, and by it slew *me.*
(12) Wherefore the law *is* holy, and the commandment holy, and just, and good.
(13) Was then that which is good made death unto me? God forbid. But sin, that it might appear sin, working death in me by that which is good; that sin by the commandment might become exceeding sinful.
(Rom. 7:7-13)

Why, then, did God put Israel under the law? God used the law to demonstrate the sin and guilt of the world. It was a schoolmaster to bring sinners to Christ.

(19) Now we know that what things soever the law saith, it saith to them who are under the law: that every mouth may be stopped, and all the world may become guilty before God.

(20) Therefore by the deeds of the law there shall no flesh be justified in his sight: for by the law *is* the knowledge of sin. (Rom. 3:19-20)

(21) *Is* the law then against the promises of God? God forbid: for if there had been a law given which could have given life, verily righteousness should have been by the law.
(22) But the scripture hath concluded all under sin, that the promise by faith of Jesus Christ might be given to them that believe.
(23) But before faith came, we were kept under the law, shut up unto the faith which should afterwards be revealed.
(24) Wherefore the law was our schoolmaster *to bring us* unto Christ, that we might be justified by faith.
(25) But after that faith is come, we are no longer under a schoolmaster. (Gal. 3:21-25)

The problem was not the law, but the inability of the flesh to keep it. The flesh cannot be justified or sanctified by keeping the law because it requires perfect obedience (Gal. 3:10).

(14) For we know that the law is spiritual: but I am carnal, sold under sin.
(15) For that which I do I allow not: for what I would, that do I not; but what I hate, that do I.
(16) If then I do that which I would not, I consent unto the law that *it is* good.
(17) Now then it is no more I that do it, but sin that dwelleth in me.
(18) For I know that in me (that is, in my flesh,) dwelleth no good thing: for to will is present with me; but *how* to perform that which is good I find not. (Rom. 7:14-18)

The law appeals to the flesh because the pride of man deceives him into thinking he can be righteous by doing the works it requires. The Spirit will lead us to put our trust in Christ and His righteousness. God gives us by grace what we could never earn in our flesh.

(1) *There is* therefore now no condemnation to them which are in Christ Jesus, who walk not after the flesh, but after the Spirit.
(2) For the law of the Spirit of life in Christ Jesus hath made me free from the law of sin and death.
(3) For what the law could not do, <u>in that it was weak through the flesh</u>, God sending his own Son in the likeness of sinful flesh, and for sin, condemned sin in the flesh:
(4) That the righteousness of the law might be fulfilled in us, who walk not after the flesh, but after the Spirit.
(Rom. 8:1-4)

Many who preach salvation by grace teach the Christian life as a performance-based system (Gal. 3:3). They try to use the law to get believers to live right. The law does not stop or even hinder sin (Rom. 6:14; 1 Cor. 15:56). How did Israel do under the law? They failed miserably, and we have the same corrupt flesh that they did.

What it Means to Be Under Grace

Being under grace does not give us a "license to sin" as some ignorantly claim.

What then? shall we sin, because we are not under the law, but under grace? God forbid. (Rom. 6:15)

God did not put us under grace because He decided to lower, or even eliminate, His standard of righteousness. He put us under grace to enable us by His Spirit to live righteously in Christ. Grace is not liberty TO sin, but liberty FROM sin (Rom. 6:7, 18, 22).

Living under grace is about living the Christ-life (Gal. 2:20). Spiritual growth is about Christ being formed in us (Gal. 4:19). Those who walk in the Spirit do not need the law.

(22) But the fruit of the Spirit is love, joy, peace, longsuffering, gentleness, goodness, faith,
(23) Meekness, temperance: <u>against such there is no law</u>.
(Gal. 5:22-23)

The answer to legalism is not liberalism. There are many today who talk much about being under grace, but instead of living under grace, they are trying to make grace be under their carnal desires. They try to use grace as an alibi for living worldly and accuse any preacher who exhorts believers to live a separated and holy life unto God of being a legalist.

What does it mean to live under grace? To be "under" something is to be in a state of:
1) Indebtedness (Rom. 8:12-13) – Being under grace does not free us from responsibility.
2) Tutelage (Titus 2:11-15) – Being under grace does not excuse ignorance.
3) Governance (1 Cor. 15:10) – Being under grace is not freedom from authority.

Those who desire to be under the law instead of grace understand neither.

Chapter 8
Review Questions

1. Under the law, God's blessings were based on the _____ of His people. Under grace, His blessings are _____ to us in the Lord Jesus Christ.

2. What is the problem with the law?

3. Why does the law appeal to the flesh?

4. Grace is not liberty ____ sin, but liberty _____ sin.

5. What does the grace of God teach us (Titus 2:11-12)?

Chapter 9
Standing and State

The moment we trust Jesus Christ as our Saviour we are complete in Him. There is nothing we can do to add or take away from being complete in Christ.

And <u>ye are complete in him</u>, which is the head of all principality and power: (Col. 2:10)

Yet, in the same epistle we find prayers being offered for believers to stand complete in all the will of God. There were believers at Colosse who were not standing for the truth of being complete in Christ because they were listening to false teachers who were seeking to rob them of that blessing (Col. 2:8-10).

Epaphras, who is *one* of you, a servant of Christ, saluteth you, always labouring fervently for you in prayers, <u>that ye may stand perfect and complete in all the will of God</u>. (Col. 4:12)

This seeming contradiction, and others, are cleared up when we understand the difference between the believers standing and state. Failure to understand this difference will result in confusion and problems.

- **Standing** = Our unchangeable position based on who we are in Christ.

Study Notes

(1) Therefore being justified by faith, we have peace with God through our Lord Jesus Christ:
(2) By whom also we have access by faith into this grace wherein we stand, and rejoice in hope of the glory of God. (Rom. 5:1-2)

(3) Know ye not, that so many of us as were baptized into Jesus Christ were baptized into his death?
(4) Therefore we are buried with him by baptism into death: that like as Christ was raised up from the dead by the glory of the Father, even so we also should walk in newness of life. (Rom. 6:3-4)

(4) But God, who is rich in mercy, for his great love wherewith he loved us,
(5) Even when we were dead in sins, hath quickened us together with Christ, (by grace ye are saved;)
(6) And hath raised *us* up together, and made *us* sit together in heavenly *places* in Christ Jesus:
(7) That in the ages to come he might shew the exceeding riches of his grace in *his* kindness toward us through Christ Jesus. (Eph. 2:4-7)

For ye are dead, and your life is hid with Christ in God. (Col. 3:3)

- **State** = Our changeable condition based on our walk.

If we live in the Spirit, let us also walk in the Spirit. (Gal. 5:25)

For ye were sometimes darkness, but now *are ye* light in the Lord: walk as children of light: (Eph. 5:8)

Not that I speak in respect of want: for I have learned, in whatsoever state I am, *therewith* to be content. (Phil. 4:11)

What we learned in the previous two chapters is related to the issue of our standing and state. The reason that our state does not always line up with our standing is due to the fact we have two natures. In this present age all believers are under grace, but sadly many are trying to live under the law in their state.

The goal in spiritual growth is to get our state lined up more and more with our standing. In other words, we must learn to live out by faith who we are in Christ. Our state does not affect our standing, but our standing should affect our state.

(12) Wherefore, my beloved, as ye have always obeyed, not as in my presence only, but now much more in my absence, work out your own salvation with fear and trembling.
(13) For it is God which worketh in you both to will and to do of *his* good pleasure. (Phil. 2:12-13)

There is a perfect balance in Paul's epistles between the believers standing and state. His pattern was to begin with sound doctrine concerning our standing and then make the proper application of that doctrine to our state. We must not focus on one to the exclusion of the other because they go together. For example, the first three chapters of Ephesians concern our standing as members of the Body of Christ, and the last three chapters concerns our state.

Notice in the following passage (Col. 3:1-17) how Paul applies our standing to our state.

STANDING
(1) If ye then be risen with Christ,

STATE
seek those things which are above, where Christ sitteth on the right hand of God.
(2) Set your affection on things above, not on things on the earth.

STANDING
(3) For ye are dead, and your life is hid with Christ in God.
(4) When Christ, *who is* our life, shall appear, then shall ye also appear with him in glory.

STATE
(5) Mortify therefore your members which are upon the earth; fornication, uncleanness, inordinate affection, evil concupiscence, and covetousness, which is idolatry:
(6) For which things' sake the wrath of God cometh on the children of disobedience:
(7) In the which ye also walked some time, when ye lived in them.
(8) But now ye also put off all these; anger, wrath, malice, blasphemy, filthy communication out of your mouth.
(9) Lie not one to another, seeing that ye have put off the old man with his deeds;

STANDING

(10) And have put on the new *man*, which is renewed in knowledge after the image of him that created him:

(11) Where there is neither Greek nor Jew, circumcision nor uncircumcision, Barbarian, Scythian, bond *nor* free: but Christ *is* all, and in all.

STATE

(12) Put on therefore, as the elect of God, holy and beloved, bowels of mercies, kindness, humbleness of mind, meekness, longsuffering;

(13) Forbearing one another, and forgiving one another, if any man have a quarrel against any: even as Christ forgave you, so also *do* ye.

(14) And above all these things *put on* charity, which is the bond of perfectness.

(15) And let the peace of God rule in your hearts, to the which also ye are called in one body; and be ye thankful.

(16) Let the word of Christ dwell in you richly in all wisdom; teaching and admonishing one another in psalms and hymns and spiritual songs, singing with grace in your hearts to the Lord.

(17) And whatsoever ye do in word or deed, *do* all in the name of the Lord Jesus, giving thanks to God and the Father by him.

Let's apply what we have learned concerning our standing and state to three areas of our Christian life.

1) Sanctification

To be sanctified is to be set apart for God. All believers are sanctified in Christ, but that should also be evident in our walk.

STANDING
And such were some of you: but ye are washed, but ye are sanctified, but ye are justified in the name of the Lord Jesus, and by the Spirit of our God. (1 Cor. 6:11)

STATE
Having therefore these promises, dearly beloved, let us cleanse ourselves from all filthiness of the flesh and spirit, perfecting holiness in the fear of God. (2 Cor. 7:1)

2) Service

All believers are accepted in Christ, but our service may not be accepted at the Judgment Seat of Christ (more about this in the last chapter). Salvation is a free gift, but rewards are earned by faithful service.

STANDING
To the praise of the glory of his grace, wherein he hath made us accepted in the beloved. (Eph. 1:6)

STATE
(9) Wherefore we labour, that, whether present or absent, we may be accepted of him.
(10) For we must all appear before the judgment seat of Christ; that every one may receive the things *done* in *his* body, according to that he hath done, whether *it be* good or bad. (2 Cor. 5:9-10)

3) Security

It is possible for a believer to be deceived and moved away from the truth, but it is impossible to lose salvation.

(15) Study to shew thyself approved unto God, a workman that needeth not to be ashamed, rightly dividing the word of truth.

(16) But shun profane *and* vain babblings: for they will increase unto more ungodliness.

(17) And their word will eat as doth a canker: of whom is Hymenaeus and Philetus;

STATE

(18) Who concerning the truth have erred, saying that the resurrection is past already; and overthrow the faith of some.

STANDING

(19) Nevertheless the foundation of God standeth sure, having this seal, The Lord knoweth them that are his. And, Let every one that nameth the name of Christ depart from iniquity. (2 Tim. 2:15-19)

Chapter 9
Review Questions

1. Our standing refers to our _____ before God.

2. Our state refers to our _____ based on our walk.

3. The goal in spiritual growth is to get our _____ lined up more and more with our _____.

4. Do the following verses refer to our standing or state?
   - 1 Cor. 6:11 _____
   - 2 Cor. 7:1 _____
   - Eph. 1:6 _____
   - 2 Cor. 5:9 _____

Chapter 10
The Will of God

It is not possible to overemphasize the importance of knowing and doing the will of God. Sadly, many believers have been led to believe that finding the will of God is a very difficult task. God has not hidden His will. If He did, we would never find it! Thankfully, the Lord wants us to understand His will and be filled with the knowledge of it.

(15) See then that ye walk circumspectly, not as fools, but as wise,
(16) Redeeming the time, because the days are evil.
(17) Wherefore be ye not unwise, but understanding what the will of the Lord *is*. (Eph 5:15-17)

(9) For this cause we also, since the day we heard *it*, do not cease to pray for you, and to desire that ye might be filled with the knowledge of his will in all wisdom and spiritual understanding;
(10) That ye might walk worthy of the Lord unto all pleasing, being fruitful in every good work, and increasing in the knowledge of God; (Col. 1:9-10).

Consider the serious consequences of NOT knowing the will of God:
1) We will be unwise and walk as fools, wasting precious time.

2) We will be unable to walk worthy of the Lord and we will be unfruitful.

We can know the will of God. The question is, how do we find it? We DO NOT find the will of God by:
1) Signs (1 Cor. 1:22)
2) Feelings (Prov. 28:26; Jer. 17:9)
3) Circumstances (Phil. 4:11-13)

God speaks to us through His word (2 Tim. 3:16-17). We must rely completely on His word to know His will. That is a simple answer, but we must keep a couple of things in mind.

1. All of the Bible is FOR our learning (2 Tim. 3:16), but it was not all written TO us (2 Tim. 2:15).

Therefore, what was God's will for Israel under the dispensation of law may not be His will for the Body of Christ under grace. For example, it was God's will for Israel to offer animal sacrifices, but if a believer tried to do that today he would be out of God's will. Also, the fact that Israel is God's earthly people (given a land and promised a kingdom on earth) and the Body of Christ is His heavenly people (seated with Christ in heavenly places and blessed with all spiritual blessings in heavenly places) means that there are differences in His overall will for these groups. It is dangerous to pull scripture out of context and say, "This is God's will for me."

God's will for this present age is plainly stated in Paul's first epistle to Timothy.

Who will have all men to be saved, and to come unto the knowledge of the truth. (1 Tim. 2:4)

All who believe the gospel of Christ are instantly baptized by the Spirit into the Body of Christ (1 Cor. 12:13). As members of the Body of Christ we must learn about our standing in Christ, and then walk by faith in that truth.

God revealed the truth about the Body of Christ through the apostle Paul. Therefore, the thirteen books (Romans – Philemon) that Paul wrote by inspiration of God to the Body of Christ is the source we must go to in order to know the will of God for this present age. The Lord has even revealed the mystery of His will concerning our inheritance in the eternal state (Eph. 1:9-11).

So, first of all, as we go the scripture to find God's will, we must be careful to rightly divide the word of truth if we are going to know God's will for this present age. There is another thing we must keep in mind as we go to the scripture to find God's will.

2. We should focus on the big picture of the revealed will of God and not on the details of our life.

As we study the Bible, we should note the passages in which the will of God is clearly stated. You will learn that God clearly reveals His will concerning the main issues of life. If we stay focused on doing the revealed will of God, the details of what we should do on a daily basis will start falling into place. In fact, once we know God's will for the present age and His revealed will for us as individual Christians, we will be able to easily make the right decisions concerning the details of life.

Examples of the revealed will of God:
1) Separation unto God (Rom. 12:1-2)
2) Give ourselves unto God (2 Cor. 8:5)
3) Seek to be filled with the Spirit (Eph. 5:17-21)
4) Work as unto Christ (Eph. 6:5-8)
5) Sanctification (1 Thess. 4:3; 5:23)
6) Prayer and Thanksgiving (1 Thess. 5:17-18)
7) Evangelism (1 Tim. 2:1-7)

As sons of God, we have the liberty to make decisions that will glorify God (Gal. 4:1-7). The details of what we are to do are not all spelled-out in Paul's epistles like it was for Israel who were treated as little children under the law. The Bible does not teach that every detail of our life was predetermined and planned by God before the foundation of the world.

When it comes to the unrevealed will of God, we must base our decisions on scriptural principles:
1) Does it glorify God (1 Cor. 10:31)?
2) Is it spiritually edifying (1 Cor. 10:23)?
3) Is it expedient (i.e., useful, profitable) to my Christian growth (1 Cor. 6:12)?
4) Can it bring me under bondage (1 Cor. 6:12)?
5) Will it be a hindrance to others (1 Cor. 8:9)?

When it comes to the will of God, our biggest problem is not knowing it, but doing it. We must learn to do God's will (Ps. 143:10) because the flesh naturally wants to do its own will. With the privilege of knowing God's will comes the responsibility to do it. We can only do the will of God by His power working in us (Phil. 2:13).

Chapter 10
Review Questions

1. We will NOT find the will of God by:
    1) _____
    2) _____
    3) _____

2. We must rely completely on _____ to know God's will.

3. All of the Bible is _____ our learning (2 Tim. 3:16), but it was not all written _____ us (2 Tim. 2:15).

4. List three examples of the revealed will of God.
    1) _____
    2) _____
    3) _____

5. List two scriptural principles that help us make the right decisions.
    1) _____
    2) _____

Chapter 11
Our Commission

Why didn't the Lord just take us home to heaven when He saved us? Why did He leave us in this evil world? He left us here as His ambassadors to tell others how they too can be saved.

(17) Therefore if any man *be* in Christ, *he is* a new creature: old things are passed away; behold, all things are become new.
(18) And all things *are* of God, who hath reconciled us to himself by Jesus Christ, and hath given to us the ministry of reconciliation;
(19) To wit, that God was in Christ, reconciling the world unto himself, not imputing their trespasses unto them; and hath committed unto us the word of reconciliation.
(20) Now then we are ambassadors for Christ, as though God did beseech *you* by us: we pray *you* in Christ's stead, be ye reconciled to God.
(21) For he hath made him *to be* sin for us, who knew no sin; that we might be made the righteousness of God in him. (2 Cor. 5:17-21)

This passage contains the Lord's commission to the Body of Christ for this present age of grace (note the word "committed" in v.19). All who are "IN Christ" (v.17) are "ambassadors FOR Christ" (v.20).

In the Bible there are various commissions given by God for different dispensations. Therefore, we must be clear on which one we are to labor under.

Most consider the commission found at the end of the Gospels and the beginning of Acts (Matt. 28:19-20; Mk. 16:15-18; Lk. 24:45-49; Jn. 20:21-23; Acts 1:8) to be our "Great Commission." It is commonly taught that these were the last words of Christ to His church. However, after Christ ascended to Heaven, He later appeared to Saul of Tarsus (who became the apostle Paul), saved him by grace, and sent him to the world with a new message and ministry.

The "Great Commission" is a kingdom commission for Israel. The Body of Christ had not been revealed when Christ commissioned His Jewish apostles.

Kingdom Commission	Grace Commission
Gospel of the kingdom (Matt. 24:14)	Gospel of the grace of God (Acts 20:24)
Water baptism required (Mk. 16:16)	Paul not sent to baptize (1 Cor. 1:17)
Signs of the kingdom (Mk. 16:17-18)	Signs ceased (1 Cor. 13:8-13)
Begin in Jerusalem (Lk. 24:47; Acts 1:8)	Depart from Jerusalem (Acts 22:21)
Teach the law (Matt. 5:17-20; 28:20)	Not under the law (Rom. 6:14)

Failure to rightly divide (2 Tim. 2:15) the different commissions will result in great confusion and problems. Sadly, many churches today are trying in vain to fulfill the wrong commission.

The Meaning

What does it mean to be an ambassador? An ambassador is one who is sent to a foreign country to represent his home country. As believers we are seated with Christ in "heavenly places" (Eph. 2:6) and this world is not our home. We are to represent Christ by shining as lights in the world (Phil. 2:15).

Ambassadors:
1) **They are sent in a time of peace** – We are living in the "day of salvation" (2 Cor. 6:2). The "day of his wrath" (Rev. 6:17) will not come until after this age ends.
2) **They represent their king and homeland** – We are here in "Christ's stead." Christ is working in the world through the members of His Body, the church. We should desire for Christ to be made manifest in our life (2 Cor. 4:10-11).
3) **An important message is committed to them** (Prov. 13:17) – Paul said, "we were allowed of God to be put in TRUST with the gospel" (1 Thess. 2:4).
4) **They are brought home before war is declared** – Christ will take His church off the earth before the tribulation period begins (1 Thess. 5:9).

The Message

We have been given the "ministry of reconciliation" which means that it is our responsibility to give out the "word of reconciliation" that has been "committed unto us." Who better to give the message of reconciliation than those who have been reconciled to God?

Reconciliation is to bring two disputing parties together. Lost sinners are "enemies of God" (Rom. 5:10). God has done a work that enables Him to bring lost sinners into a right relationship with Him.

How did God make reconciliation possible?

- **"God was in Christ"** – When Christ shed His blood on the cross it was the pure blood of God (Acts 20:28).
- **"reconciling the world unto himself"** – He did a work through His death, burial, and resurrection (1 Cor. 15:3-4) that made it possible for the world to be saved. Christ died for ALL (2 Cor. 5:14). God will not accept man's attempts at reconciliation (religion). He has been sinned against and He alone sets the terms for reconciliation.
- **"not imputing their trespasses unto them"** – The word "impute" means to put on the account of. God took the sin of the world and put it on His Son (2 Cor. 5:21). Christ willingly died for our sins (2 Cor. 5:18; Rom. 5:10; Col. 1:21-22).
- **"that we might be made the righteousness of God in Him"** – Those who receive the offer of reconciliation by faith have the righteousness of Christ imputed to them.

God has made reconciliation possible for the world, but it is not applied to a sinner unless he believes the gospel. Reconciliation is not automatic otherwise there would be no need for us to "beseech" sinners to "be reconciled to God."

Those who are reconciled to God are made a "new creature." Upon salvation we are baptized by the Spirit into the Body of Christ. Our identity is in Him and therefore the old things of the flesh are passed away and all things are new (2 Cor. 5:16). In Christ there is no fleshly distinctions, such as Jew and Gentile, but we are made one in Him (Gal. 3:27-28).

The Ministry

God is not presently dealing with the world in wrath as He will in the future tribulation period. He desires to "beseech" sinners through us to be reconciled to Him. To "beseech" is to ask or plead with urgency. We are to let sinners know that reconciliation to God is available and simply "pray" them (i.e., ask them) to believe the gospel. It is not our responsibility to save sinners, but it is our responsibility to tell them how to be saved.

Learning how to share the gospel comes by experience. To get started, use gospel tracts, and share your testimony as you have opportunity. The power is in the gospel (Rom. 1:16), not in our ability to present it.

The basics of the gospel:
1) All have sinned and there is none righteous (Rom. 3:10, 23).
2) We deserve death and hell for our sins (Rev. 21:8).
3) We cannot be saved by any works that we do (Titus 3:5).
4) Jesus Christ died on the cross for our sins, was buried, and rose again the third day (1 Cor. 15:3-4).
5) We are saved by grace through faith in the finished work of Christ (Eph. 2:8-9).

God does not want us to make the church worldly in an effort to draw the lost to our building. The local church is about saved people being edified in the truth of God's word. We are to go out into the world to reach the lost. We are not to depend on gimmicks and tricks to get a crowd. The Spirit of God and the word of God is all we need to do the work of the ministry.

The Motive

What will motivate us to be faithful ambassadors for Christ? In 2 Corinthians 5 the apostle Paul reveals his motives in the ministry. For example, we must give an account of our ministry at the judgment seat of Christ (2 Cor. 5:9-11). Perhaps the greatest motivation is the love of Christ.

(14) For the love of Christ constraineth us; because we thus judge, that if one died for all, then were all dead:
(15) And *that* he died for all, that they which live should not henceforth live unto themselves, but unto him which died for them, and rose again. (2 Cor. 5:14-15)

When we consider the price Christ paid to save sinners because of His great love, it should motivate us to get His message out to a lost and dying world. Christ made the greatest sacrifice to accomplish salvation; we should be willing to sacrifice time and money to make it known.

Chapter 11
Review Questions

1. List three differences between the kingdom commission of Israel and the commission of the Body of Christ.
    1) _____
    2) _____
    3) _____

2. What does it mean to be an ambassador?

3. What is our message as ambassadors for Christ?

4. What are the basics points in presenting the gospel?
    1) _____
    2) _____
    3) _____
    4) _____
    5) _____

5. What will motivate us to be faithful ambassadors for Christ?

Chapter 12
Our Enemies

As we learned in the last chapter, God leaves us on the earth after He saves us because He has a work for us to do as His ambassadors. Those who faithfully serve the Lord should not expect it to be easy. We will face opposition in this present evil world, but the word of God enlightens us concerning who our enemies are, how they work against us, and how we may walk in victory over them.

Identifying our Enemies

(1) And you *hath he quickened,* who were dead in trespasses and sins;
(2) Wherein in time past ye walked according to the course of <u>this world</u>, according to <u>the prince of the power of the air</u>, the spirit that now worketh in the children of disobedience:
(3) Among whom also we all had our conversation in times past in the lusts of <u>our flesh</u>, fulfilling the desires of the flesh and of the mind; and were by nature the children of wrath, even as others. (Eph. 2:1-3)

We have three primary enemies, and they are mentioned together in this one passage: the world, the prince of the power of the air (Satan), and our own flesh.

Before salvation we were children of the Devil (Jn. 8:44), walking in the course of this world with our conversation (i.e., manner of life) being in the lusts of our flesh. Upon salvation we become children of God (Gal. 3:26), delivered from this present evil world (Gal. 1:4) with our conversation being in heaven (Phil. 3:20). To God be all the glory for this great difference He made in our lives (Eph. 2:4-10)! Whereas we were in-step with the world, the flesh, and the Devil, we are now in conflict with them.

1) Satan (1 Pet. 5:8) – Created in eternity past as a perfect being (Isa. 14:12-15; Ezek. 28:11-19), Lucifer lifted up his heart in pride against God and became His adversary. There is a real and literal Devil who is a king over many devils. He is destined for the lake of fire, but he is not there yet (Matt. 25:41). We may learn some basics of who he is by considering his names and titles.

For example:
- Satan (56x's in the Bible) – adversary
- Devil (34x's) – accuser
- Serpent (15x's) – deceiver
- Prince of the power of the air – rules over evil spirits
- Prince of this world (3x's) – rules over the nations
- god of this world – rules over false religion

2) World (Jn. 15:18-19) – We are not talking about the plants and animals, or all the people who live on the earth. We are talking about the evil world system that Satan uses against God and His people. When Adam fell into sin Satan usurped the dominion that God gave man on the earth. Satan is behind the politics and religion of this "present evil world."

3) Flesh (Rom. 7:18) – The flesh refers to our corrupt human nature. Upon salvation we receive a new nature by the Spirit of God, but our flesh remains corrupt. When we

give place to the flesh, we also give place to the world and the Devil (Eph. 4:27).

Satan's Strategy

Satan is not omniscient (all-knowing), omnipresent (everywhere present), and omnipotent (all-powerful) like God is, but he is a formidable adversary that we cannot handle in our own strength. If we are ignorant of how Satan works, it gives him a great advantage over us (2 Cor. 2:11).

Satan's strategy against man remains basically the same as it was in the Garden of Eden because it has been effective.

But I fear, lest by any means, as the serpent beguiled Eve through his subtilty, so your minds should be corrupted from the simplicity that is in Christ. (2 Cor. 11:3)

(1) Now the serpent was more subtil than any beast of the field which the LORD God had made. And he said unto the woman, Yea, hath God said, Ye shall not eat of every tree of the garden?
(2) And the woman said unto the serpent, We may eat of the fruit of the trees of the garden:
(3) But of the fruit of the tree which *is* in the midst of the garden, God hath said, Ye shall not eat of it, neither shall ye touch it, lest ye die.
(4) And the serpent said unto the woman, Ye shall not surely die:
(5) For God doth know that in the day ye eat thereof, then your eyes shall be opened, and ye shall be as gods, knowing good and evil.
(6) And when the woman saw that the tree *was* good for food, and that it *was* pleasant to the eyes, and a tree to be

desired to make *one* wise, she took of the fruit thereof, and did eat, and gave also unto her husband with her; and he did eat. (Gen. 3:1-6)

- **"subtil"** – Sly, artful, crafty, deceitful.
- **"Yea"** – The first word that Satan says to mankind is positive. Watch out for smooth talkers (Rom. 16:18)!
- **"hath God said"** – Satan will always cast doubt on what God said (cf. Matt. 4:3).
- **"Ye shall not eat of every tree of the garden?"** – He changed what God said (Gen. 2:16-17). God did not say "Ye shall NOT eat of every tree" but "of every tree of the garden thou mayest FREELY eat: but of the tree of the knowledge of good and evil thou shalt not eat of it."
- **"Ye shall not surely die"** – Once he brings doubt on God's word, he replaces it with a lie. Notice that he simply added ONE word ("not") to what God said in Gen. 2:17 (Prov. 30:5-6)
- **"For God doth know that in the day ye eat thereof"** – He slanders God's character by suggesting that He was holding back something good from her.
- **"then your eyes shall be opened, and ye shall be as gods"** – He appeals to pride which was his own downfall (1 Tim. 3:6).
- **"knowing good and evil"** – There is always an element of truth in deception.
- **"good for food... pleasant to the eyes... desired to make one wise"** – Satan tempts from the outside in: body, soul, and spirit (1 Jn. 2:16).

Satan's strategy:
1) Appear as something he is not (2 Cor. 11:14)
2) Start positive
3) Cast doubt on what God said

4) Change what God said
5) Replace the truth with a lie (Jn. 8:44)
6) Slander God's character
7) Appeal to pride

The apostle Paul warned the Body of Christ again and again about the danger of **spiritual deception** (e.g., 1 Tim. 4:1; 2 Tim. 3:13).

It is God's will for all men to be saved and come to the knowledge of the truth (1 Tim. 2:4). Therefore, it is Satan's will to:
1) Blind sinners to the gospel of the grace of God – by counterfeit gospels that add human works (2 Cor. 4:3-4; 11:4; Gal. 1:6-12).
2) Blind saints to the mystery of the Body of Christ – by the mystery of iniquity (2 Thess. 2:7), which is Satan's religious system.

Dealing with Temptation

(13) Let no man say when he is tempted, I am tempted of God: for God cannot be tempted with evil, neither tempteth he any man:
(14) But every man is tempted, when he is drawn away of his own lust, and enticed.
(15) Then when lust hath conceived, it bringeth forth sin: and sin, when it is finished, bringeth forth death.
(Jam. 1:13-15)

Paul referred to Satan as "the tempter" (1 Thess. 3:5). Temptation is about getting us to fulfill lawful desires in an unlawful way. For example, it is not a sin to be hungry, but gluttony is a sin. In every temptation there is a way to escape. It is not a sin to be tempted, but it is a sin to yield to temptation.

Keys to defeating temptation:
1) Believe and obey the word of God (Matt. 4:1-11)
2) Walk in the Spirit (Gal. 5:16)
3) Make no provision for the flesh (Rom. 13:14)
4) Flee the temptation (1 Cor. 6:18; 10:14; 1 Tim. 6:11; 2 Tim. 2:22)

Victory in Christ

As to our standing in Christ, we have the victory over the world, the flesh, and the Devil. But as to our state, it is possible for believers to be worldly, carnal, and deceived. Believers cannot lose salvation, but they can and be taken captive by the snare of the Devil (2 Tim. 2:26). Satan is a defeated foe (Heb. 2:14), but his final execution is yet future (Rom. 16:20).

In order to walk in victory over the world, the flesh, and the Devil, we must put on the whole armour of God.

(10) Finally, my brethren, be strong in the Lord, and in the power of his might.
(11) Put on the whole armour of God, that ye may be able to stand against the wiles of the devil.
(12) For we wrestle not against flesh and blood, but against principalities, against powers, against the rulers of the darkness of this world, against spiritual wickedness in high places.
(13) Wherefore take unto you the whole armour of God, that ye may be able to withstand in the evil day, and having done all, to stand.

**(14) Stand therefore, having your loins girt about with truth, and having on the breastplate of righteousness;
(15) And your feet shod with the preparation of the gospel of peace;
(16) Above all, taking the shield of faith, wherewith ye shall be able to quench all the fiery darts of the wicked.
(17) And take the helmet of salvation, and the sword of the Spirit, which is the word of God:
(18) Praying always with all prayer and supplication in the Spirit, and watching thereunto with all perseverance and supplication for all saints;
(19) And for me, that utterance may be given unto me, that I may open my mouth boldly, to make known the mystery of the gospel,
(20) For which I am an ambassador in bonds: that therein I may speak boldly, as I ought to speak.** (Eph. 6:10-20)

Consider some highlights from this great passage:
1) Notice how Paul called it the WHOLE armour of God. He mentions seven pieces (the number of perfection). If we leave off a piece, Satan will find that opening.
2) It is God's responsibility to provide the armor, but it is our responsibility to put it on.
3) A spiritual war against spiritual enemies requires spiritual weapons (2 Cor. 10:3-6). The Bible is our main offensive weapon. With this sharp sword we may cut spiritual enemies (Heb. 4:12). That God promised to provide us with the sword of the Spirit proves that we still have the inspired word of God today. Satan hates the word of God and has attacked it from the beginning. He wants to replace our sharp sword with something else. Most professing Christians today are using a butter knife in the form of corrupt modern versions, instead of a two-edged sword, the pure King James Bible. Among those that use

the sword of the Spirit, many do not know how to handle it (2 Tim. 2:15). With the sword of the Spirit, we may: defeat temptation, evangelize the lost, and build believers up in the faith.
4) To put on this spiritual armor is to put on Christ (Rom. 13:11-14). We must have the armor of light to fight against spiritual darkness. As to our standing, we put on Christ the moment of salvation. But as to our state, we must put on Christ by faith in our daily walk.
5) Every piece is connected to the word of God. The central piece is the shield of faith because it is believing the word that activates the armor (Prov. 30:5-6).

There is much more to learn in the Bible about our enemies. It is vital that we understand how they work against us, and how we can walk in victory over them. Failure to take our enemies seriously will have serious consequences.

Chapter 12
Review Questions

1. List our three main enemies.
   1) _____
   2) _____
   3) _____

2. Satan's strategy is always to cast doubt on _____.

3. The apostle Paul warned the Body of Christ again and again about the danger of _____.

4. What are the keys to defeating temptation?
   1) _____
   2) _____
   3) _____
   4) _____

5. To walk in victory over the world, the flesh, and the Devil, we must put on the _____.

6. Why is the shield of faith the central piece of the armour?

Chapter 13
Suffering

There is a popular false teaching which claims that those who are right with God will always enjoy good health and financial prosperity. That is not what the word of God teaches and believing it will only set you up for major disappointment and discouragement.

The apostle Paul, who was right with God, had much to say about suffering in his epistles. He was an expert on the subject because he not only wrote by inspiration of God, but he also suffered like few people have in this world.

(23) Are they ministers of Christ? (I speak as a fool) I *am* more; in labours more abundant, in stripes above measure, in prisons more frequent, in deaths oft.
(24) Of the Jews five times received I forty *stripes* save one.
(25) Thrice was I beaten with rods, once was I stoned, thrice I suffered shipwreck, a night and a day I have been in the deep;
(26) *In* journeyings often, *in* perils of waters, *in* perils of robbers, *in* perils by *mine own* countrymen, *in* perils by the heathen, *in* perils in the city, *in* perils in the wilderness, *in* perils in the sea, *in* perils among false brethren;

(27) In weariness and painfulness, in watchings often, in hunger and thirst, in fastings often, in cold and nakedness. (2 Cor. 11:23-27)

Of course, none have ever, or will ever, suffer more than the Lord Jesus Christ did. He is not a far-off God who does not understand what we are going through (Heb. 4:15).

The Reality of Suffering

For I reckon that the sufferings of this present time *are* not worthy *to be compared* with the glory which shall be revealed in us. (Rom. 8:18)

Paul took it for granted that we will suffer in this life. Unlike the celebrity preachers of today, Paul did not ignore the reality of suffering or make people vainly think they could somehow escape it. We will all have physical infirmities. We will all have heartaches and distress. We will all have burdens to bear. Since suffering is a reality that we all must face, it would be wise to learn how to deal with it.

The Reasons for Suffering

(22) For we know that the whole creation groaneth and travaileth in pain together until now.
(23) And not only *they,* but ourselves also, which have the firstfruits of the Spirit, even we ourselves groan within ourselves, waiting for the adoption, *to wit,* the redemption of our body. (Rom. 8:22-23)

Study Notes

The fundamental reason for suffering is that we live in a fallen world with fallen bodies. The only requirement to experience suffering is to be born.

Man *that is* born of a woman *is* of few days, and full of trouble. (Job 14:1)

We bring more trouble and suffering upon ourselves and those around us when we make the wrong choices.

(7) Be not deceived; God is not mocked: for whatsoever a man soweth, that shall he also reap.
(8) For he that soweth to his flesh shall of the flesh reap corruption; but he that soweth to the Spirit shall of the Spirit reap life everlasting. (Gal. 6:7-8)

When we get saved and start serving God, it does not remove or even lessen our suffering. Those who are faithful to God and the truth of His word will suffer persecution in this present evil world.

For unto you it is given in the behalf of Christ, not only to believe on him, but also to suffer for his sake; (Phil. 1:29)

(1) Wherefore when we could no longer forbear, we thought it good to be left at Athens alone;
(2) And sent Timotheus, our brother, and minister of God, and our fellowlabourer in the gospel of Christ, to establish you, and to comfort you concerning your faith:
(3) That no man should be moved by these afflictions: for yourselves know that we are appointed thereunto.

(4) For verily, when we were with you, we told you before that we should suffer tribulation; even as it came to pass, and ye know. (1 Thess. 3:1-4)

For therefore we both labour and suffer reproach, because we trust in the living God, who is the Saviour of all men, specially of those that believe. (1 Tim. 4:10)

Yea, and all that will live godly in Christ Jesus shall suffer persecution. (2 Tim. 3:12)

Sadly, many believers wrongly think that suffering is God's way of punishing us. God is FOR us, and not against us.

(31) What shall we then say to these things? If God *be* for us, who *can be* against us?
(32) He that spared not his own Son, but delivered him up for us all, how shall he not with him also freely give us all things?
(33) Who shall lay any thing to the charge of God's elect? *It is* God that justifieth.
(34) Who *is* he that condemneth? *It is* Christ that died, yea rather, that is risen again, who is even at the right hand of God, who also maketh intercession for us.
(35) Who shall separate us from the love of Christ? *shall* tribulation, or distress, or persecution, or famine, or nakedness, or peril, or sword?
(36) As it is written, For thy sake we are killed all the day long; we are accounted as sheep for the slaughter.
(37) Nay, in all these things we are more than conquerors through him that loved us.

(38) For I am persuaded, that neither death, nor life, nor angels, nor principalities, nor powers, nor things present, nor things to come,
(39) Nor height, nor depth, nor any other creature, shall be able to separate us from the love of God, which is in Christ Jesus our Lord. (Rom. 8:31-39)

The Results of Suffering

The results of suffering in our life will depend on how we choose to respond. It can help make us bitter or better. Satan is a liar and a slanderer. He wants us to blame God for all of our problems.

The book of Genesis opens with a man in paradise, but it closes with a dead man in a coffin down in Egypt. What happened (see Gen. 3)? Adam willfully chose to sin against God and thereby brought sin and death into the world (Rom. 5:12)? Why doesn't God put a stop to it? He will, but in order to do that He must get rid of sinners. In the meantime, He offers eternal life to those who will trust Him. God did not cause the fall of man, but He is using it to teach important lessons. What would we know about the love, mercy, and grace of God without the fall of man?

God does not cause our suffering, but He can use it for good **if we trust Him**. For example, here are some good things that can come out of suffering:
1) Spiritual growth and strength (Ps. 119:71; Rom. 5:1-5; 2 Cor. 1:3-7; 12:7-10; Phil. 3:10)
2) Testimony and furtherance of the gospel (Acts 16:22-31; Phil. 1:12; 4:7)
3) Eternal reward (2 Tim. 2:10-13)

The Remedy for Suffering

(24) For we are saved by hope: but hope that is seen is not hope: for what a man seeth, why doth he yet hope for?
(25) But if we hope for that we see not, *then* do we with patience wait for *it.*
(26) Likewise the Spirit also helpeth our infirmities: for we know not what we should pray for as we ought: but the Spirit itself maketh intercession for us with groanings which cannot be uttered.
(27) And he that searcheth the hearts knoweth what *is* the mind of the Spirit, because he maketh intercession for the saints according to *the will of* God.
(28) And we know that all things work together for good to them that love God, to them who are the called according to *his* purpose.
(29) For whom he did foreknow, he also did predestinate *to be* conformed to the image of his Son, that he might be the firstborn among many brethren.
(30) Moreover whom he did predestinate, them he also called: and whom he called, them he also justified: and whom he justified, them he also glorified. (Rom. 8:24-30)

The good news is that the suffering of believers is temporary (2 Cor. 4:16-18). The Bible principle is first suffering, then glory (Rom. 8:16-18). When the Lord comes, we will be glorified with Him, and our suffering will be forever over (Phil. 3:20-21).

We will not go through the prophesied tribulation period, but we will have tribulation in this life. Suffering makes the blessed hope more real in our hearts. In the meantime, God's grace is sufficient, and the Spirit helps our infirmities (Rom. 8:26-28).

Hope can carry us through the dark days. The best is yet to come!

For the lost, the suffering of this present time is nothing compared to the eternal torment they will suffer in hell if they die in their lost condition. Think of all that Christ suffered for us so that we could be saved!

Chapter 13
Review Questions

1. List three reasons that we will suffer in this world.
    1) _____
    2) _____
    3) _____

2. The results of suffering in our life will depend on how we choose to _____.

3. List three ways God can use our suffering.
    1) _____
    2) _____
    3) _____

4. When will suffering end for the Body of Christ?

Chapter 14
Our Blessed Hope

It is important to know where we are living in God's plan for the ages. The chart below provides a dispensational layout of the Bible according to the theme of the King and His Kingdom. The God of heaven will establish His kingdom on the earth (Dan. 2:44; Matt. 6:10). We are presently living in the time of the MYSTERY in which God's plan to set up His kingdom on the earth has been postponed. More information on this subject is available in our book, Study Notes on Dispensational Truth.

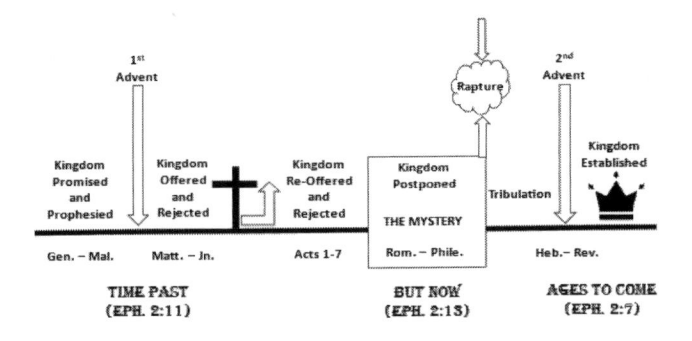

	1st Advent				Rapture		2nd Advent	Kingdom Established
Kingdom Promised and Prophesied		Kingdom Offered and Rejected		Kingdom Re-Offered and Rejected	Kingdom Postponed THE MYSTERY	Tribulation		
Gen. – Mal.		Matt. – Jn.		Acts 1-7	Rom. – Phile.		Heb. – Rev.	
TIME PAST (EPH. 2:11)					BUT NOW (EPH. 2:13)		AGES TO COME (EPH. 2:7)	

This present age of grace in which God is building the Body of Christ is a parenthetical age that interrupted His dealings with Israel and the nations. It was planned by God before the world began but it was kept secret until He first revealed it through the apostle Paul (Eph. 3:1-12). This age began with a sudden glorious appearing of Christ when He saved Paul on the road to Damascus (Acts 9) and the gospel of the grace of God came down to earth (1 Tim. 1:12-16), and it will end with another sudden glorious appearing of Christ when those who have believed that message will be caught up to heaven.

(11) For the <u>grace</u> of God that bringeth salvation hath <u>appeared</u> to all men,
(12) Teaching us that, denying ungodliness and worldly lusts, we should live soberly, righteously, and godly, in this present world;
(13) Looking for that blessed hope, and the <u>glorious</u> <u>appearing</u> of the great God and our Saviour Jesus Christ;
(14) Who gave himself for us, that he might redeem us from all iniquity, and purify unto himself a peculiar people, zealous of good works. (Titus 2:11-14)

Our Hope

Hope is a desire and expectation of something good that is yet future.

When a wicked man dieth, *his* <u>expectation</u> shall perish: and the <u>hope</u> of unjust *men* perisheth. (Prov. 11:7)

<u>Hope</u> deferred maketh the heart sick: but *when* the <u>desire</u> cometh, *it is* a tree of life. (Prov. 13:12)

According to my <u>earnest expectation</u> and *my* <u>hope</u>, that in nothing I shall be ashamed, but *that* with all boldness, as always, *so* now also Christ shall be magnified in my body, whether *it be* by life, or by death. (Phil. 1:20)

Our hope as believers is an absolute certainty because it is based on the promise of God who cannot lie (Titus 1:2). It will only become real in our hearts by faith because it concerns things that we have not seen.

(24) For we are saved by hope: but hope that is seen is not hope: for what a man seeth, why doth he yet hope for?
(25) But if we hope for that we see not, *then* do we with patience wait for *it.* (Rom. 8:24-25)

(16) For which cause we faint not; but though our outward man perish, yet the inward *man* is renewed day by day.
(17) For our light affliction, which is but for a moment, worketh for us a far more exceeding *and* eternal weight of glory;
(18) While we look not at the things which are seen, but at the things which are not seen: for the things which are seen *are* temporal; but the things which are not seen *are* eternal. (2 Cor. 4:16-18)

(For we walk by faith, not by sight:) (2 Cor. 5:7)

Now faith is the substance of things hoped for, the evidence of things not seen. (Heb. 11:1)

Our hope is Jesus Christ (1 Tim. 1:1). We are to be earnestly expecting Him to come for us to take us up to be with Him in heaven. We commonly refer to this as the "rapture," which comes from a Latin word meaning to be "caught up."

(13) But I would not have you to be ignorant, brethren, concerning them which are asleep, that ye sorrow not, even as others which have no hope.

**(14) For if we believe that Jesus died and rose again, even so them also which sleep in Jesus will God bring with him.
(15) For this we say unto you by the word of the Lord, that we which are alive *and* remain unto the coming of the Lord shall not prevent them which are asleep.
(16) For the Lord himself shall descend from heaven with a shout, with the voice of the archangel, and with the trump of God: and the dead in Christ shall rise first:
(17) Then we which are alive *and* remain shall be <u>caught up</u> together with them in the clouds, to meet the Lord in the air: and so shall we ever be with the Lord.
(18) Wherefore comfort one another with these words.** (1 Thess. 4:13-18)

For the hope which is laid up for you in heaven, whereof ye heard before in the word of the truth of the gospel; (Col. 1:5)

**(1) If ye then be risen with Christ, seek those things which are above, where Christ sitteth on the right hand of God.
(2) Set your affection on things above, not on things on the earth.
(3) For ye are dead, and your life is hid with Christ in God.
(4) When Christ, *who is* our life, shall appear, then shall ye also appear with him in glory.** (Col. 3:1-4)

It is vital that we rightly divide the word of truth (2 Tim. 2:15) and not confuse the heavenly hope of the Body of Christ with the earthly hope of Israel. The Body of Christ was a mystery (i.e., a secret) first revealed through Paul, and so was our rapture (1

Cor. 15:51). The second coming of Christ to save Israel and set up His kingdom on the earth is the subject of much prophecy, but the rapture of the Body of Christ was a mystery that is only revealed in Paul's epistles. There are many verses in the Bible that support the distinctions shown on the table below.

The Rapture	The Second Coming
Mystery revealed through Paul	Spoken by the prophets
Before the Tribulation	After the Tribulation
Christ comes secretly to meet us in the air	Christ comes publicly to earth
No signs precede	Signs precede
Christ comes in blessing	Christ comes in judgment
Christ comes for His Body	Christ comes for Israel
Judgment Seat of Christ	Judgment on Nations

Why it is a Blessed Hope

The word "blessed" in Titus 2:13 means happy. It is a source of great joy to know and believe that the best is yet to come!

Now the God of hope fill you with all joy and peace in believing, that ye may abound in hope, through the power of the Holy Ghost. (Rom. 15:13)

Our hope is a blessed hope because of:
1) **The Possibility of Escaping Death** (1 Cor. 15:51-52) - In Christ we have victory over death and therefore we should not live in the fear of it (Phil. 1:21-23). However, death is not our hope.

2) **The Certainty of Escaping Wrath** (1 Thess. 1:10; 5:9) - There are various raptures in the Bible, but our blessed hope was a mystery revealed first through Paul and is only found in his epistles. Sadly, most professing Christians are blinded to it (Eph. 1:15). The revelation of the mystery (Rom. 16:25) interrupted Israel's prophetic calendar of 70 weeks of years (Dan. 9:24-27). The 70th week of Daniel will not be fulfilled until this present age ends with the rapture. It is false doctrine to assert that the Body of Christ will go through ANY part of that prophesied seven-year tribulation period.

3) **The Joy of the Heavenly Reunion** (1 Thess. 4:13-18; 2 Thess. 2:1) - Our saved loved ones who have already died are with the Lord and we will be reunited with them in that great meeting in the air. A common question is, "Will we know our loved ones in heaven?" Yes, we will, because we will not know less than we do now.

4) **The Thrill of Seeing the Lord** (1 Tim. 6:16) - Christ laid aside His full glory, NOT His deity, when He took on flesh, but He is risen and glorified. No mortal man can see Christ in ALL His glory and live. Saul of Tarsus was blinded by just a glimpse of it (Acts 9:9). The glory of Christ is so bright it will light up the New Jerusalem for eternity (Rev. 21:10-11, 23). Being glorified we will receive a body fitted to live in His presence.

5) **The Guarantee of Glorification** (2 Cor. 5:1-8; Phil. 3:20-21) - The Spirit of God regenerated, baptized, and sealed us the moment of salvation. He is the earnest (i.e., guarantee) of the redemption of our body (Rom. 8:23; 2 Cor. 1:20-22; Eph. 1:13-14). We will receive a glorified body like Christ that will never sin, suffer, or sorrow again!

6) **The Peace of Being with the Lord** (1 Thess. 4:17-18) - This is the best part of it all! This does not mean that we will just sit at His feet forever. Since He fills heaven and earth, we will never be out of His presence no matter where we travel in the universe.

7) **The Prospect of Eternal Reward** (1 Cor. 3:10-15) - All members of the Body of Christ will be glorified, but not all will receive the same eternal rewards. Upon the rapture we must give an account of our service at the Judgment Seat of Christ (Rom. 14:10; 2 Cor. 5:10). We will not be judged for our sins because they were already judged on the cross. The issue will be the quality of our service. Did we faithfully serve the Lord according His word rightly divided, in His power, and for His glory?

Looking for Christ to Appear

That we are to be waiting and looking for Christ from heaven means that He could come at any moment (Phil. 4:5).

In his short epistle to Titus, the apostle Paul mentions "works" eight times. He makes it crystal clear that we are not saved by works (Titus 3:5), but he also makes it equally clear that those who are saved by grace should faithfully do good works (Titus 3:8; Eph. 2:8-10).

One of the great motivating factors for doing good works is the blessed hope. The Lord could appear at any moment, and we will give an account to Him of our service at the judgment seat of Christ. If the truth of the blessed hope does not affect how we live, we must not be looking for it with a sincere and believing heart.

If we love Christ, we will love His appearing. If we love His appearing, we will be looking for it daily. If we are looking for Christ to appear, we will be living in light of it.

Henceforth there is laid up for me a crown of righteousness, which the Lord, the righteous judge, shall give me at that day: and not to me only, but unto all them also that love his appearing. (2 Tim. 4:8)

(11) For the grace of God that bringeth salvation hath appeared to all men,
(12) Teaching us that, denying ungodliness and worldly lusts, we should live soberly, righteously, and godly, in this present world;
(13) Looking for that blessed hope, and the glorious appearing of the great God and our Saviour Jesus Christ;
(14) Who gave himself for us, that he might redeem us from all iniquity, and purify unto himself a peculiar people, zealous of good works. (Titus 2:11-14)

Chapter 14
Review Questions

1. What does the word "hope" mean?

2. What is the hope of the Body of Christ?

3. List three differences between the rapture of the Body of Christ and the second coming of Christ.
   1) _____
   2) _____
   3) _____

4. List three reasons that our hope is a blessed hope.
   1) _____
   2) _____
   3) _____

5. If we _____ the appearing of Christ, we will be _____ for it and _____ in light of it.

The Most Important Question

ARE YOU SAVED?

This question should receive a "Yes" or "No" answer, but it almost never does. Some of the most common responses are:
- I'm doing the best I can.
- I prayed the sinner's prayer.
- I've made Jesus the Lord of my life.
- I believe in God.
- I've been baptized.
- I'm a church member.
- I keep the commandments.
- I am basically a good person.
- I walked the aisle and prayed through.
- I've always been a Christian.
- I've never done anything really bad.

None of these responses properly answer the question. People give these kinds of responses because they evidently do not understand the question. The question, "Are you saved?" asks whether or not you have trusted Christ's shed blood on the cross as payment for your sins. It is not asking about any works that you can do. The responses listed above refer to what a person does, but salvation is only offered on the basis of Christ has already done for us.

The gospel of our salvation (Eph. 1:13) is clearly stated by the apostle Paul.

3 For I delivered unto you first of all that which I also received, how that Christ died for our sins according to the scriptures;

4 And that he was buried, and that he rose again the third day according to the scriptures. (1 Cor. 15:3-4)

The blood of Christ has purchased what we could not earn ourselves.

In whom we have redemption through his blood, even the forgiveness of sins: (Col. 1:14)

We cannot be good enough to earn salvation because "there is none righteous" (Rom. 3:10) and "all have sinned" (Rom. 3:23). The "wages of sin is death" (Rom. 6:23). Those who die lost will spend eternity in "the lake of fire" (Rev. 20:15).

In order to be saved, we must stop trusting ourselves and trust the blood payment that Christ has already made on our behalf!

8 For by grace are ye saved through faith; and that not of yourselves: it is the gift of God:
9 Not of works, lest any man should boast. (Eph. 2:8-9)

Jesus Christ fully accomplished our salvation through His death, burial, and resurrection. Therefore, the free gift of salvation can only be received by faith alone in His finished work.

Therefore being justified by faith, we have peace with God through our Lord Jesus Christ: (Rom. 5:1)

If you will trust Jesus Christ as your Saviour, you can enjoy "much assurance" (1 Thess. 1:5) that you are saved and on your way to heaven.

More From the Author

Study Notes on the King James Bible
Study Notes on Books of the Bible
Study Notes on Dispensational Truth
Study Notes on Acts
Study Notes on Romans
Study Notes on Colossians
Study Notes on the Epistles of Peter

Links to purchase the Study Notes books are found on our church website (click on Books under Resources).

For hundreds of Bible studies and messages in audio, video, and written format, please visit **www.hopebiblechurchga.com**

Hope Bible Church
199 Four Points Rd.
Jackson, GA 30233

Printed in Dunstable, United Kingdom